JOHN GRADE
DISINTEGRATION

JOHN GRADE
DISINTEGRATION
SCULPTURE THROUGH LANDSCAPE

BELLEVUE ARTS MUSEUM

COLLECTOR

WILLAPA BAY, WASHINGTON
ESCALANTE PLATEAU, UTAH
BELLEVUE, WASHINGTON

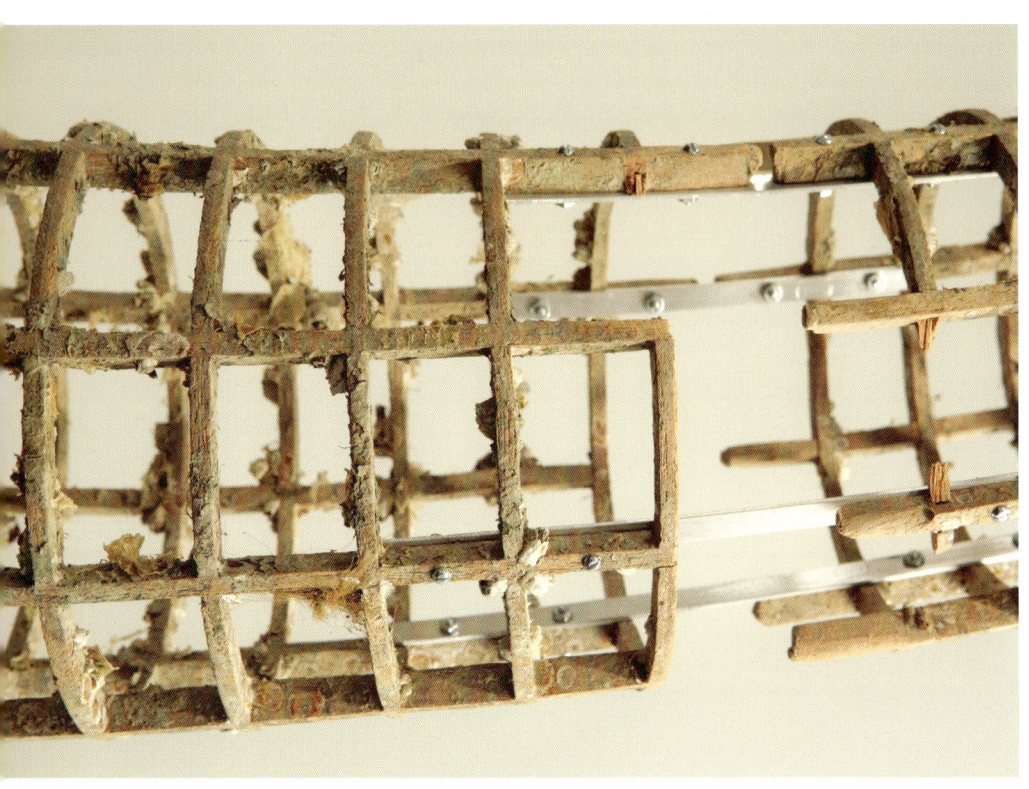

FOLD

BELLEVUE, WASHINGTON
GREAT BASIN DESERT, NEVADA (FUTURE SITE)

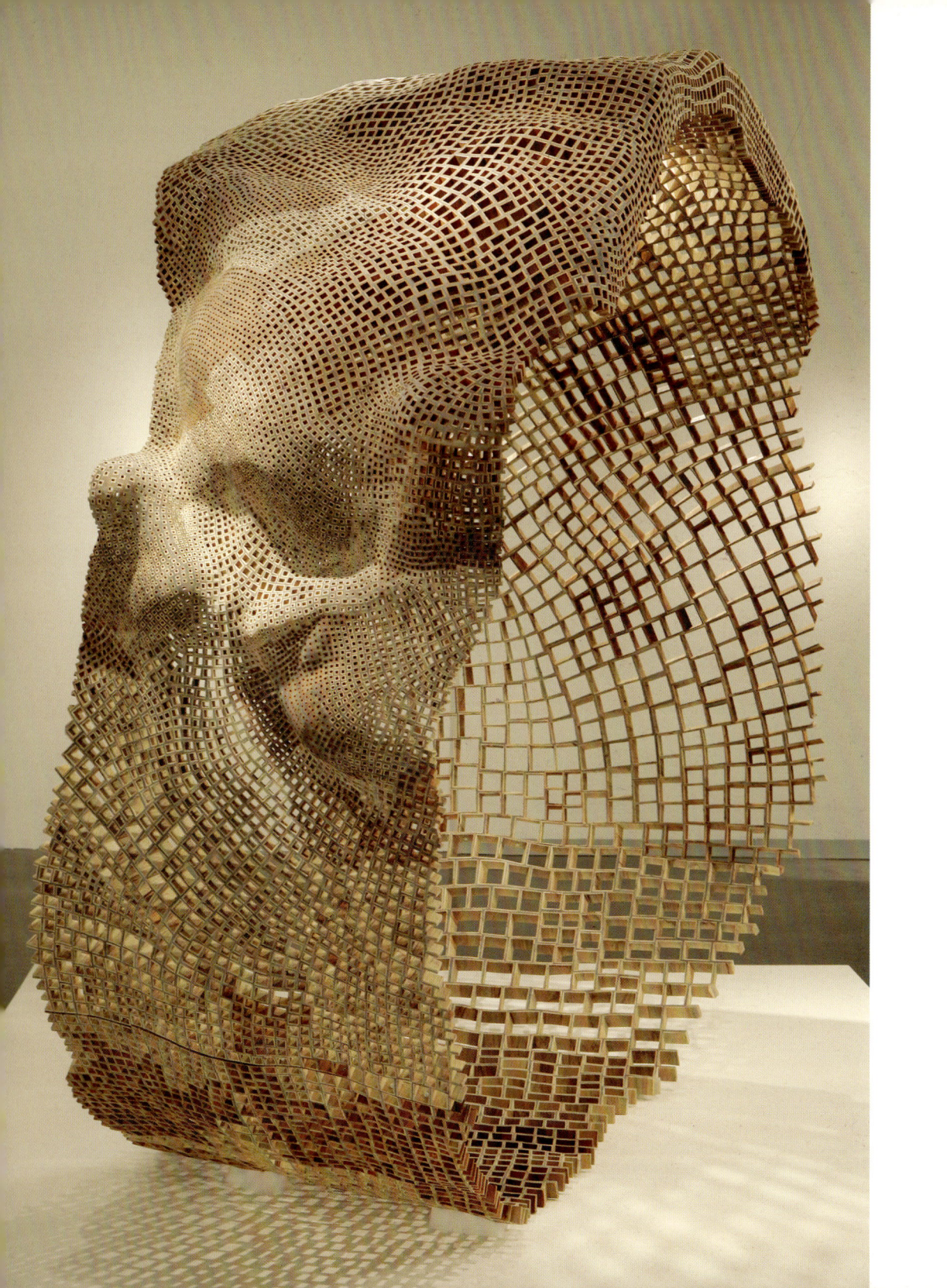

HOST

KAIBAB NATIONAL FOREST, ARIZONA

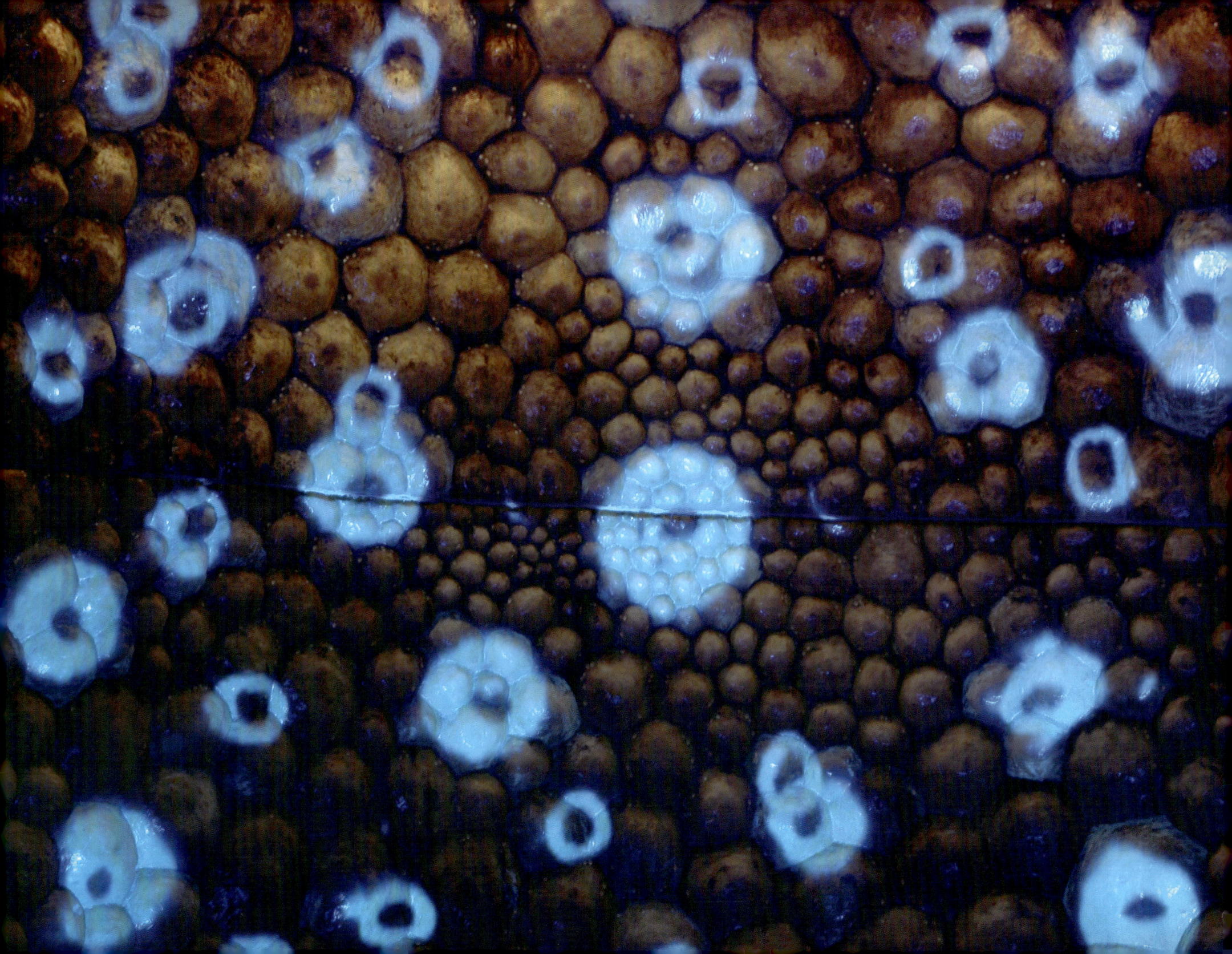

CLEAVE

SEATTLE, WASHINGTON
BELLEVUE, WASHINGTON

35

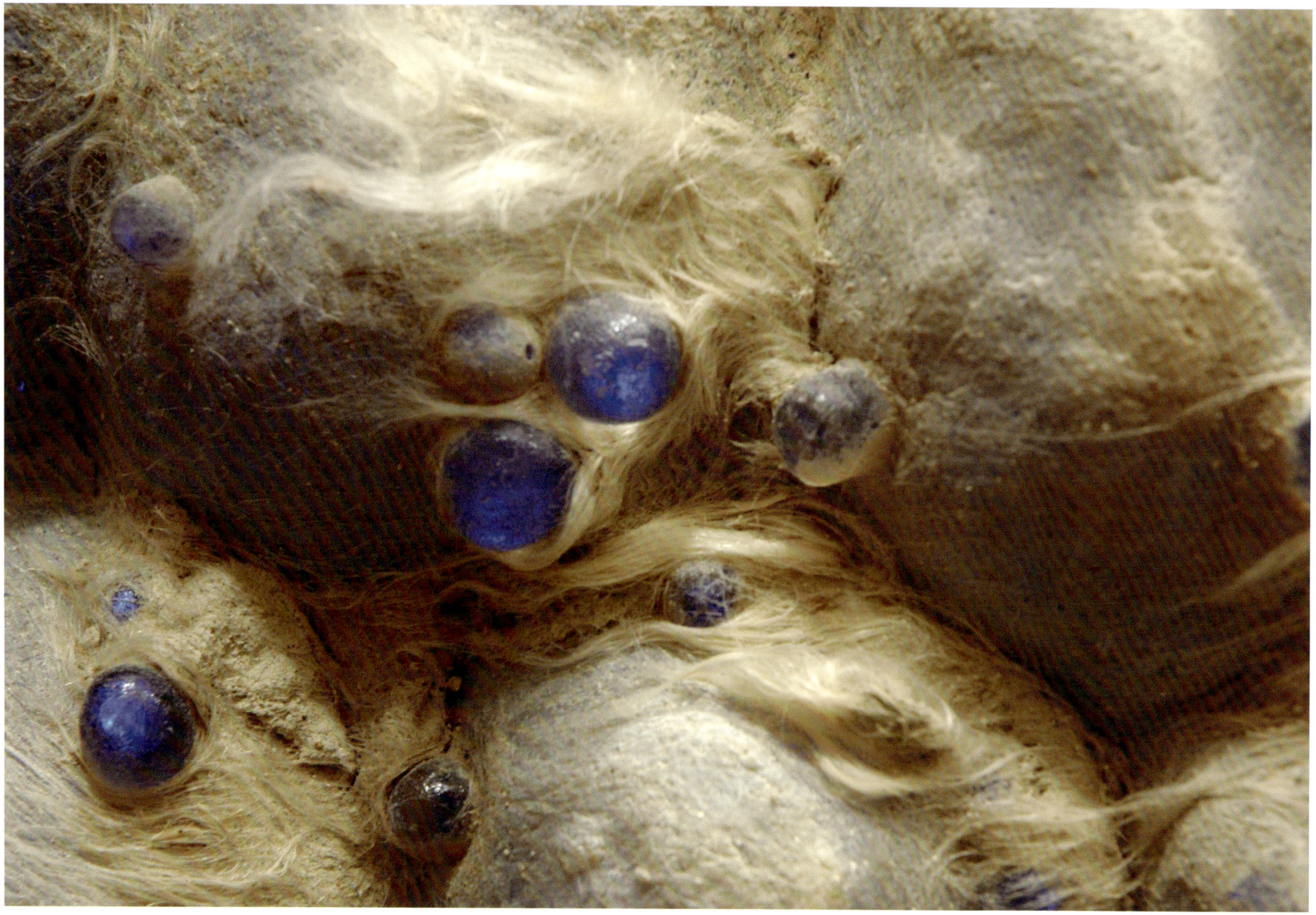

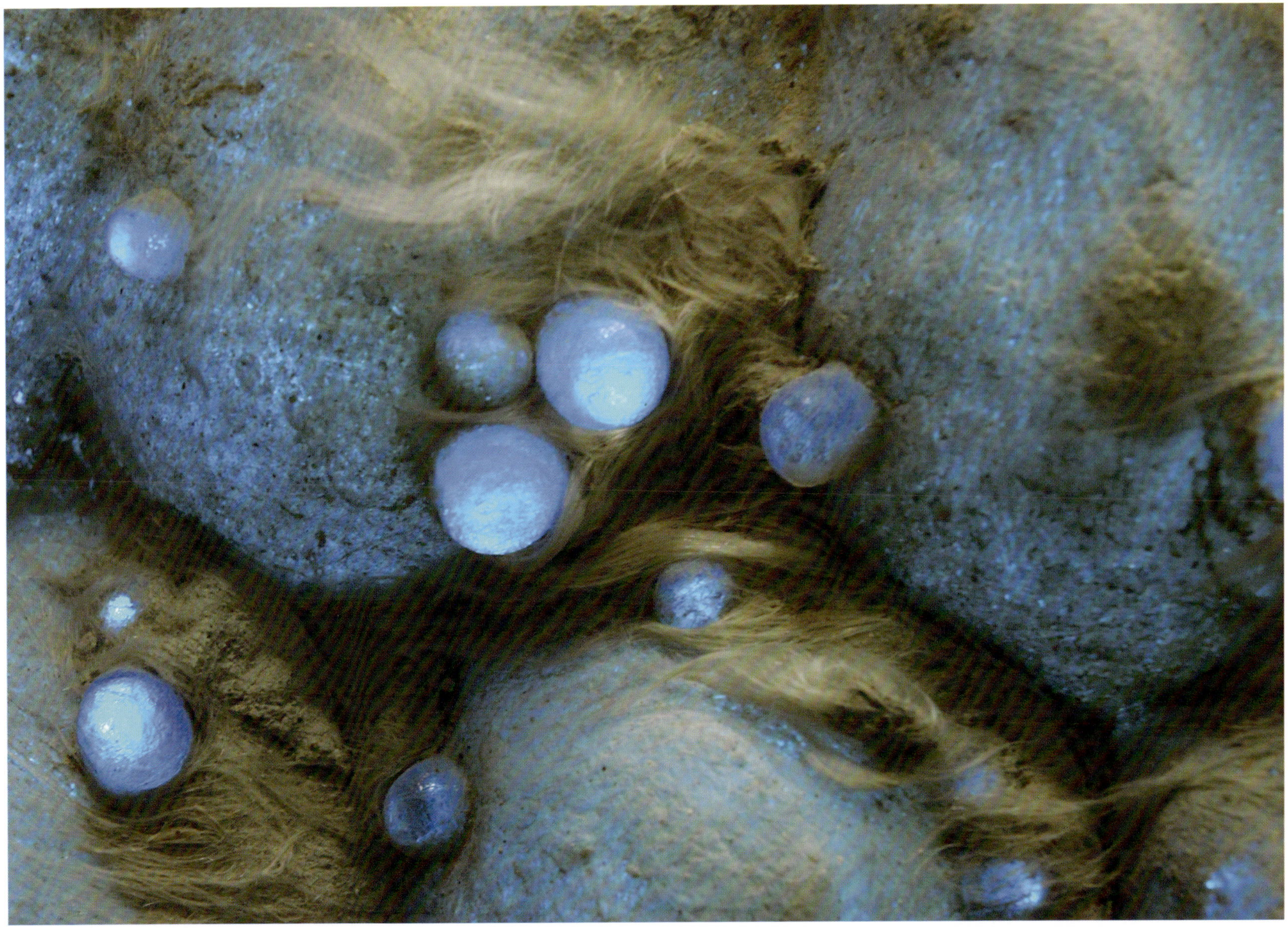

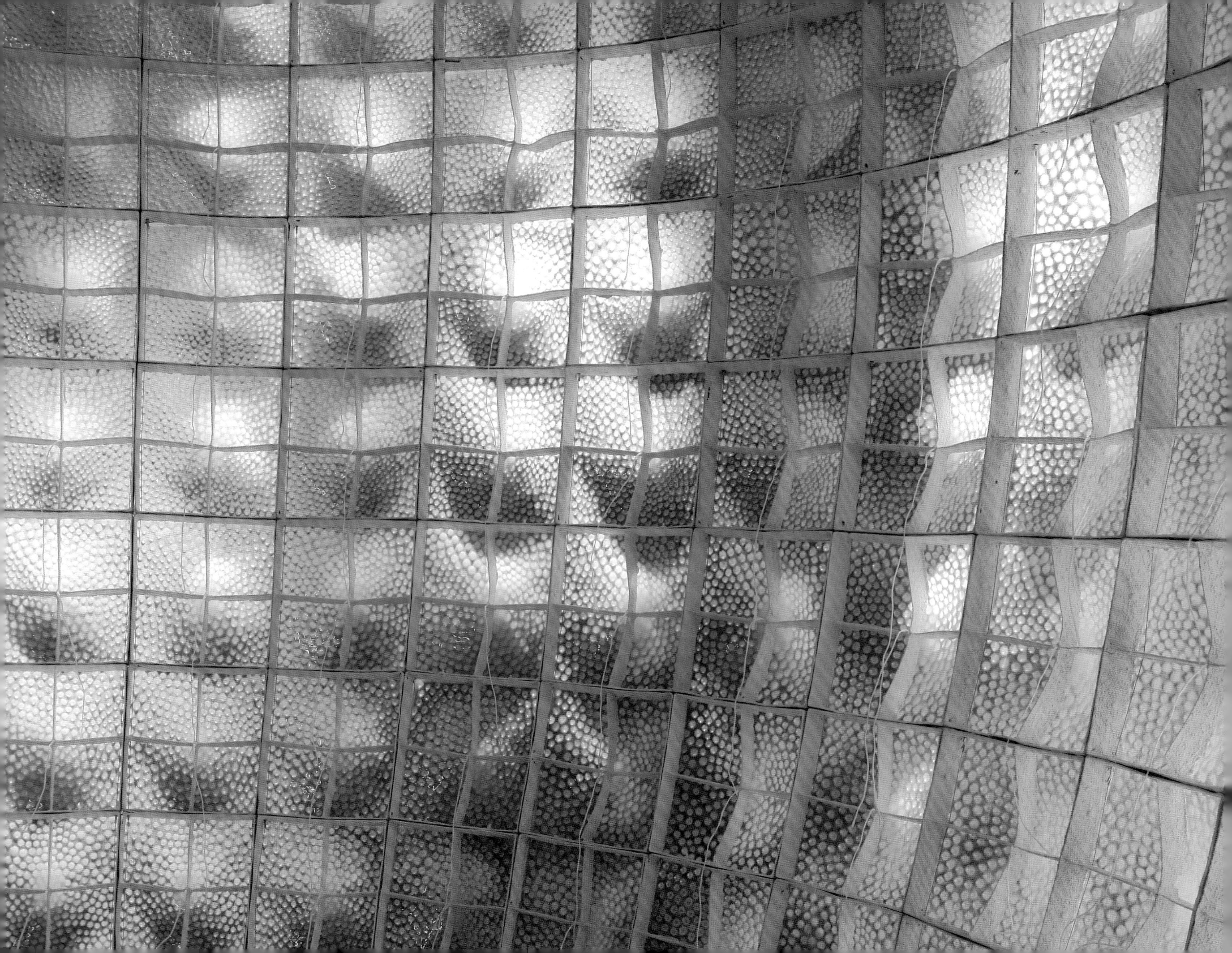

MERIDIAN

BELLEVUE, WASHINGTON
ESCALANTE PLATEAU, UTAH (FUTURE SITE)
REDWOOD FOREST, CALIFORNIA (FUTURE SITE)

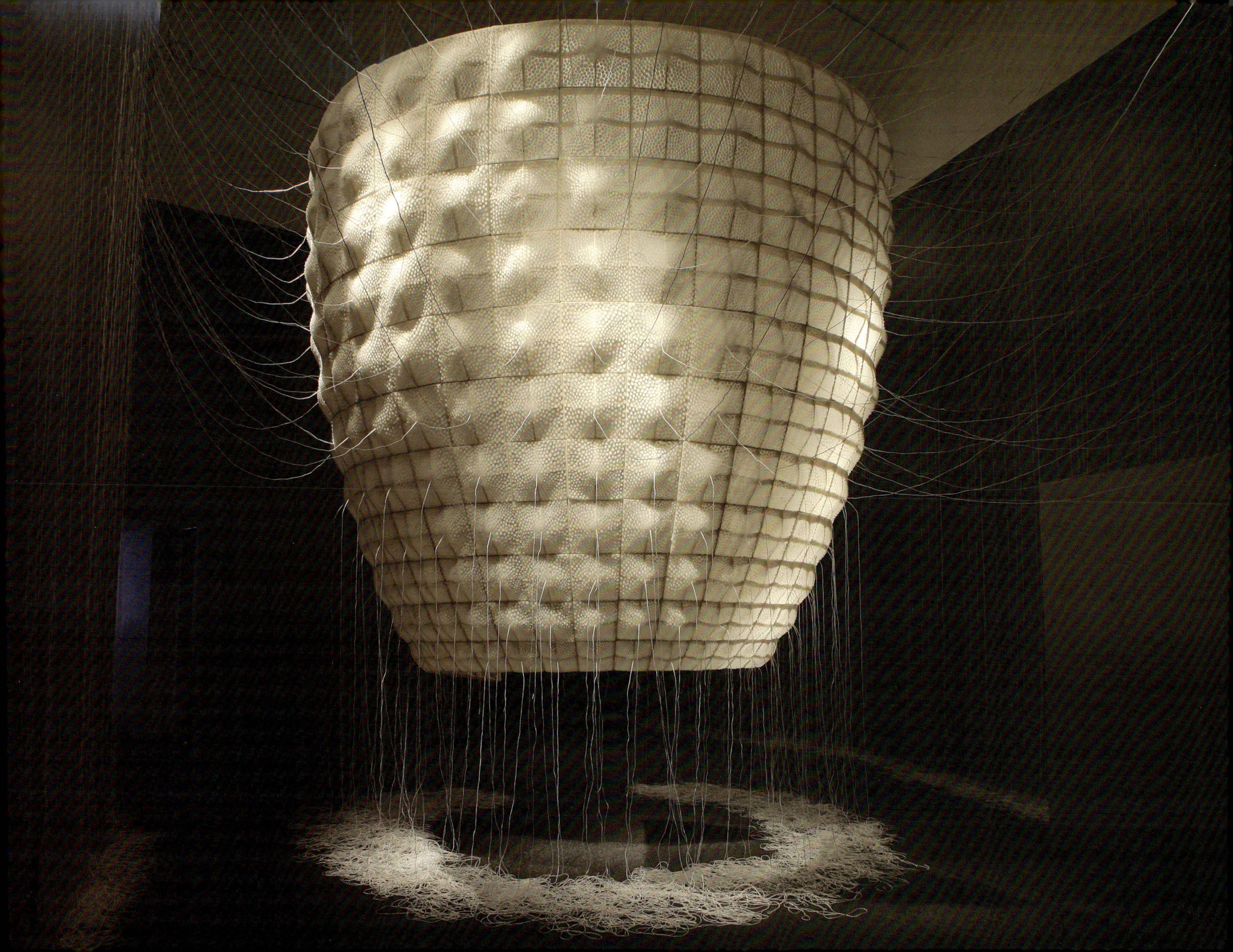

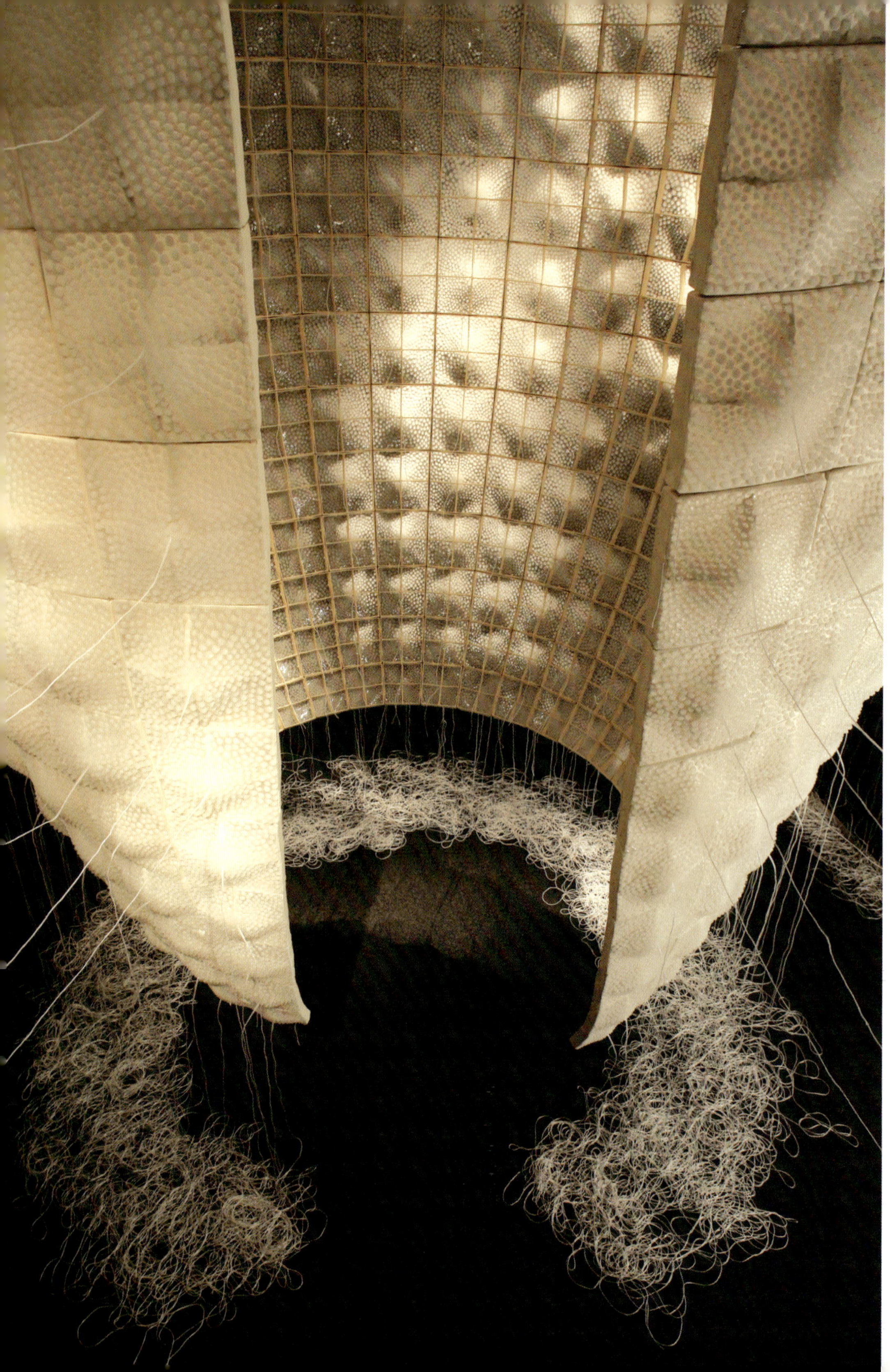

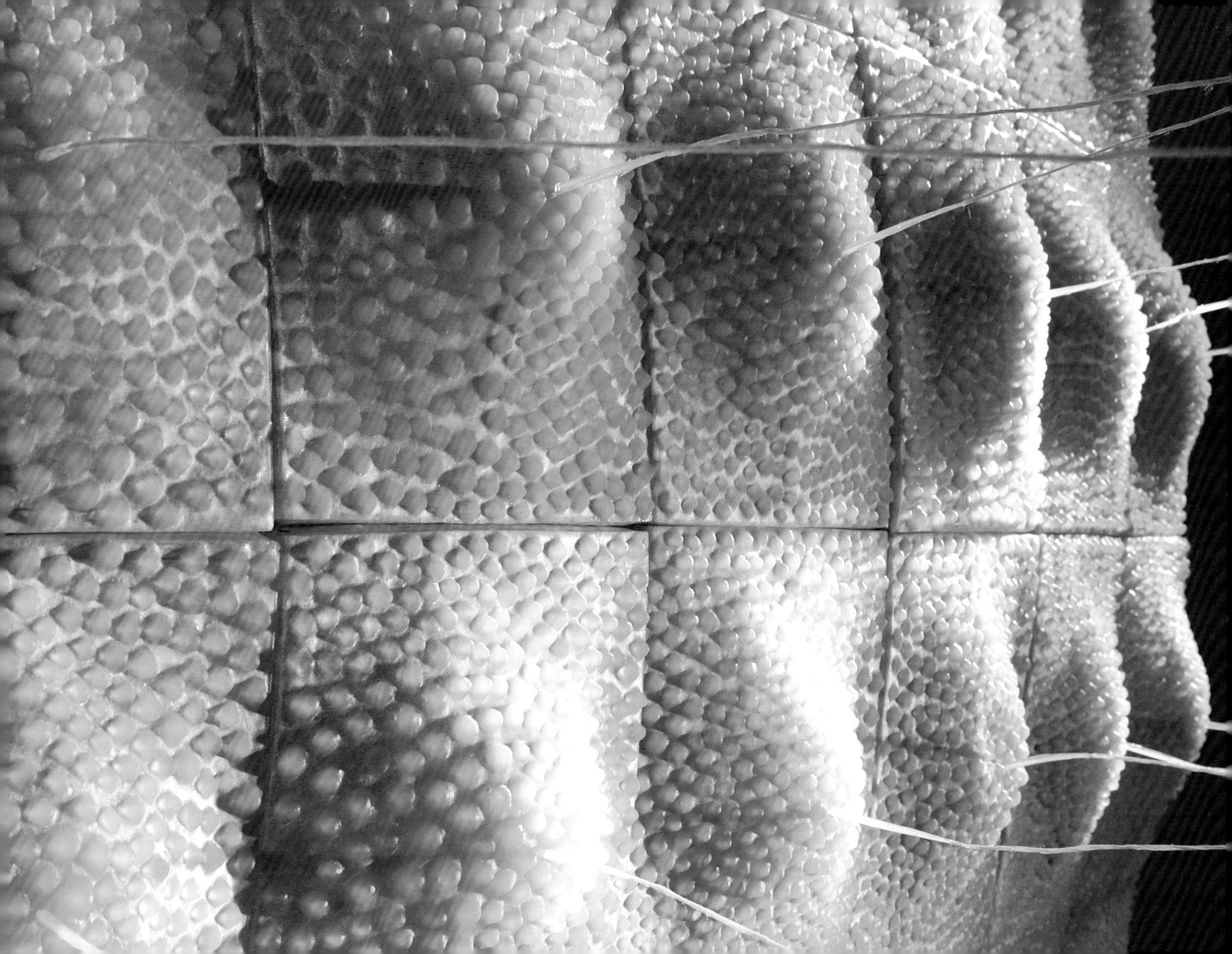

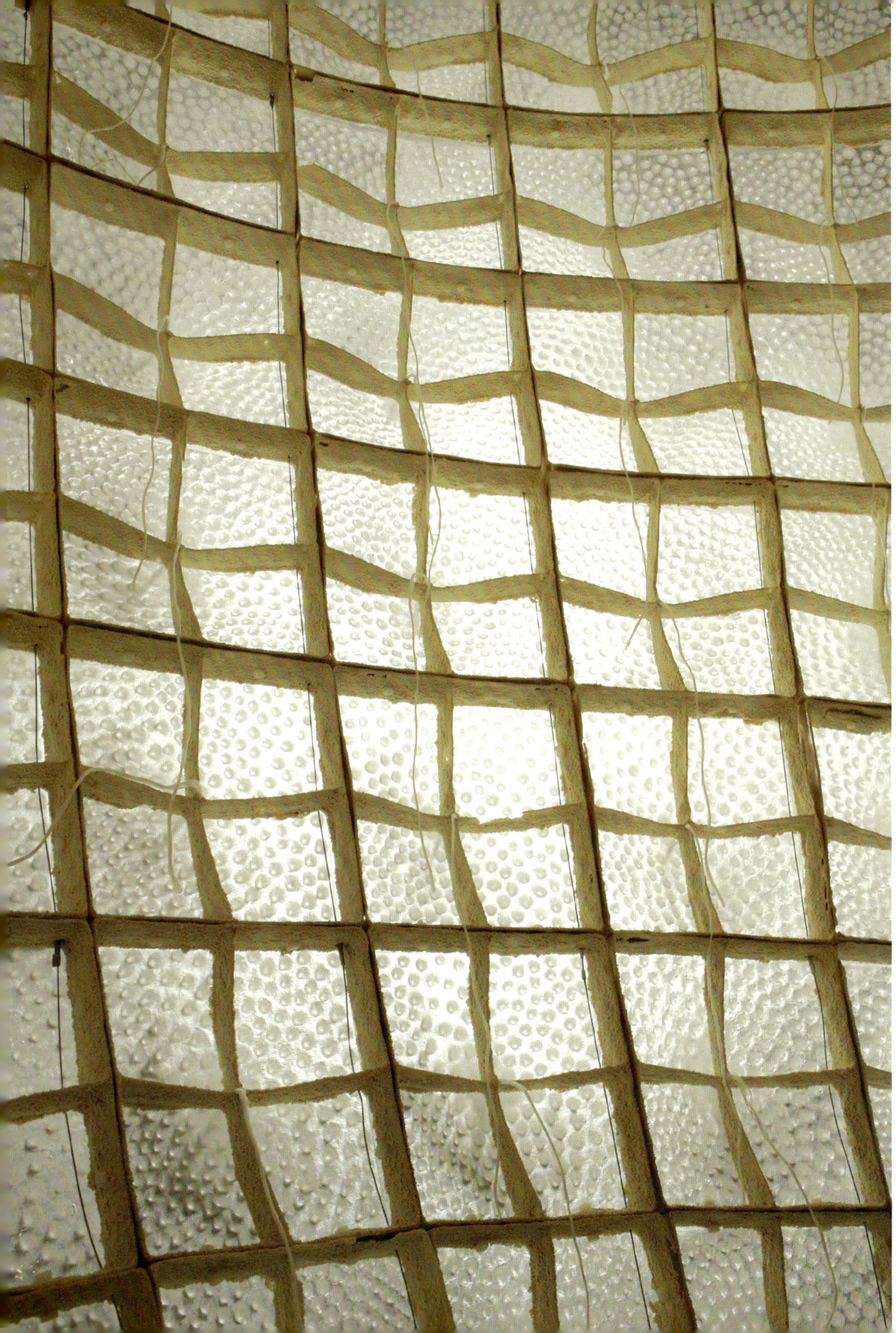

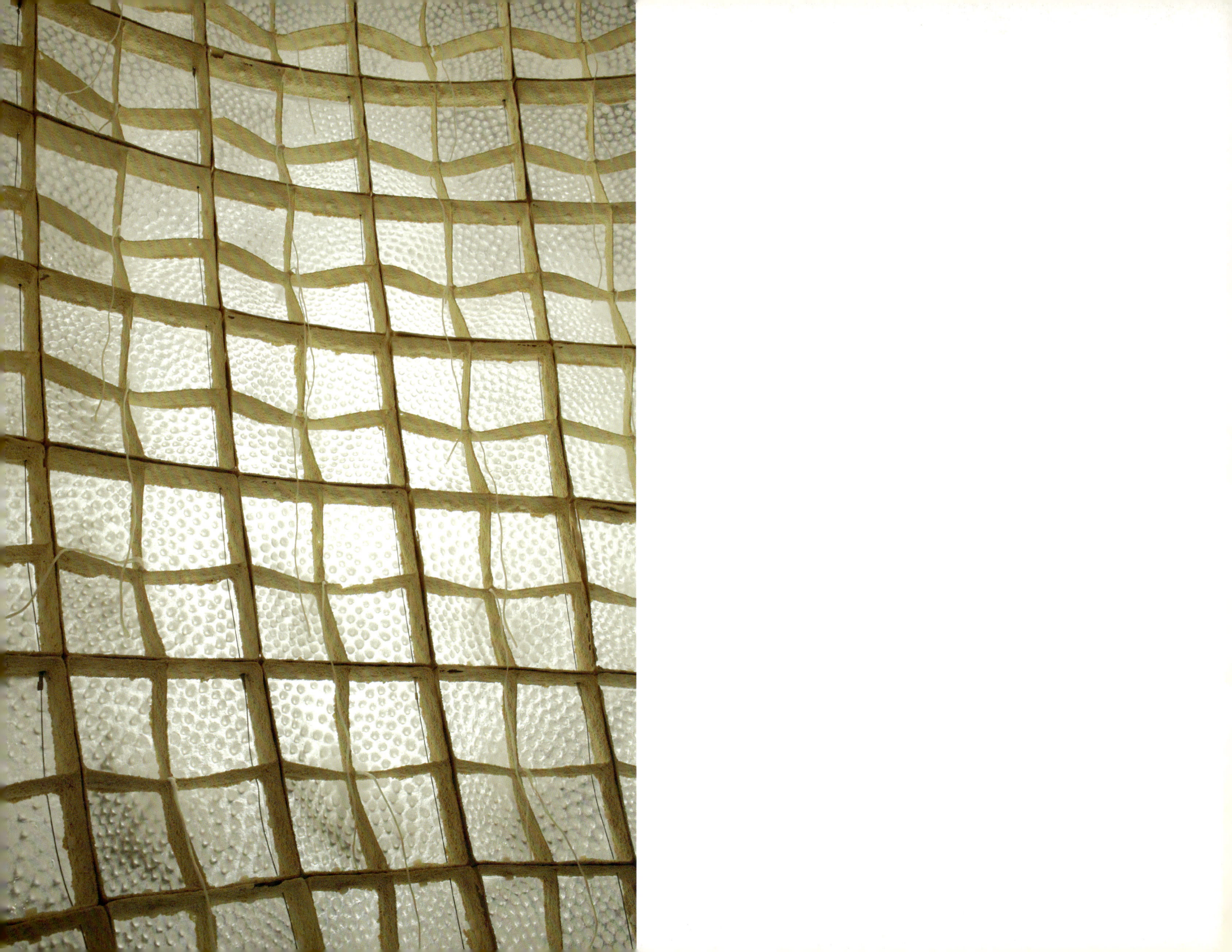

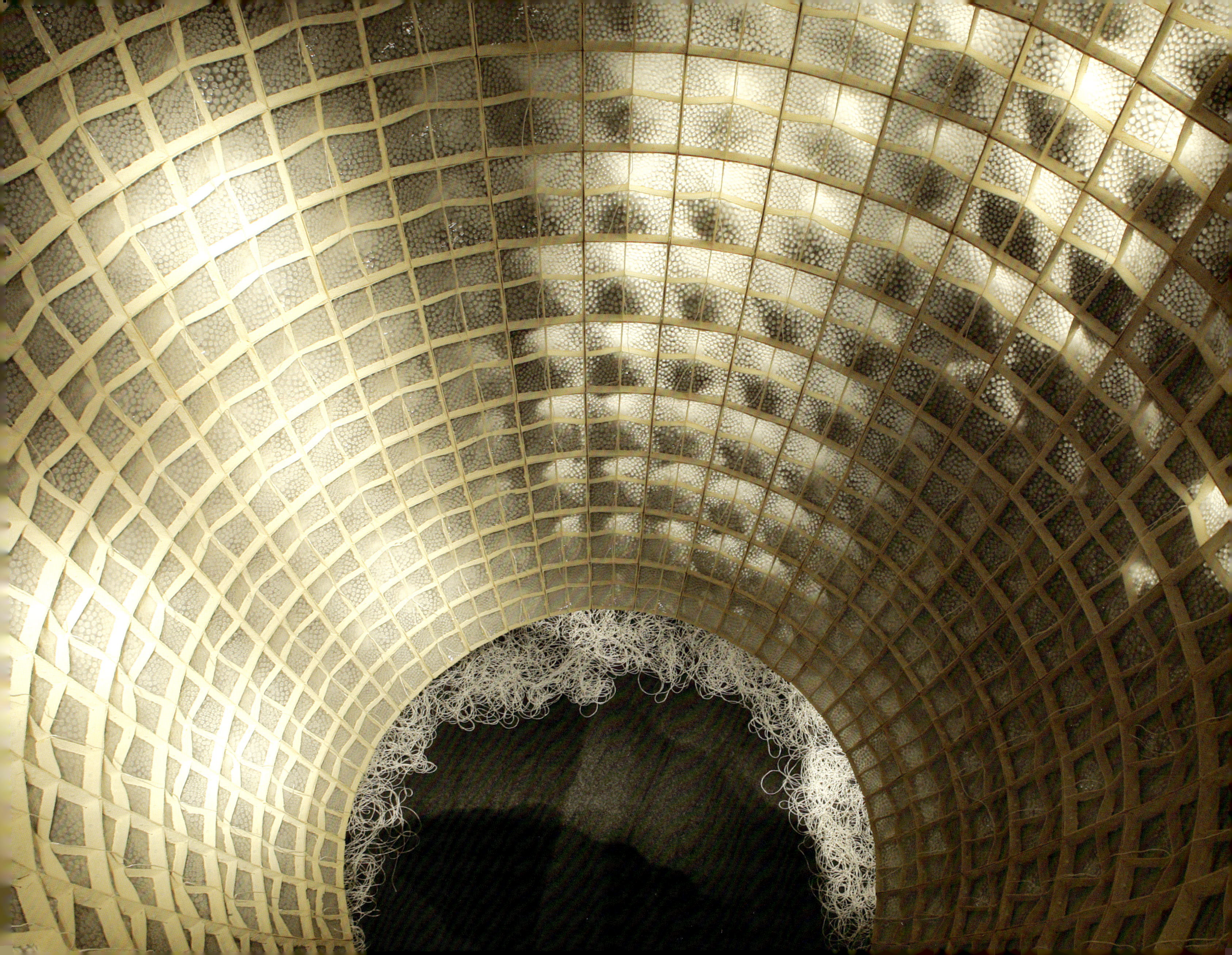

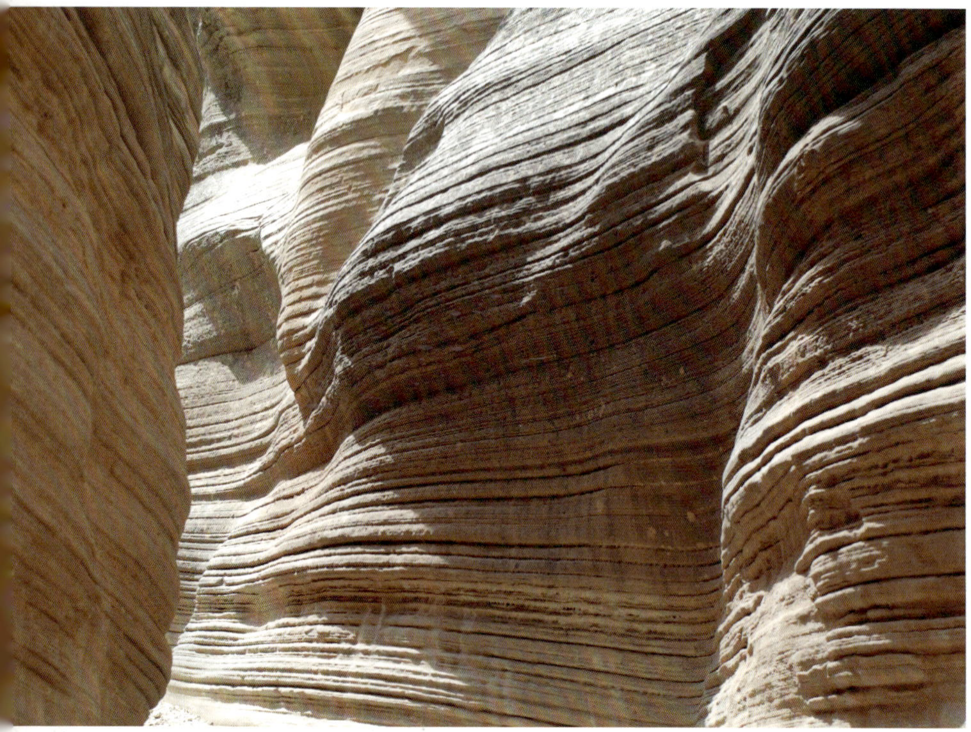

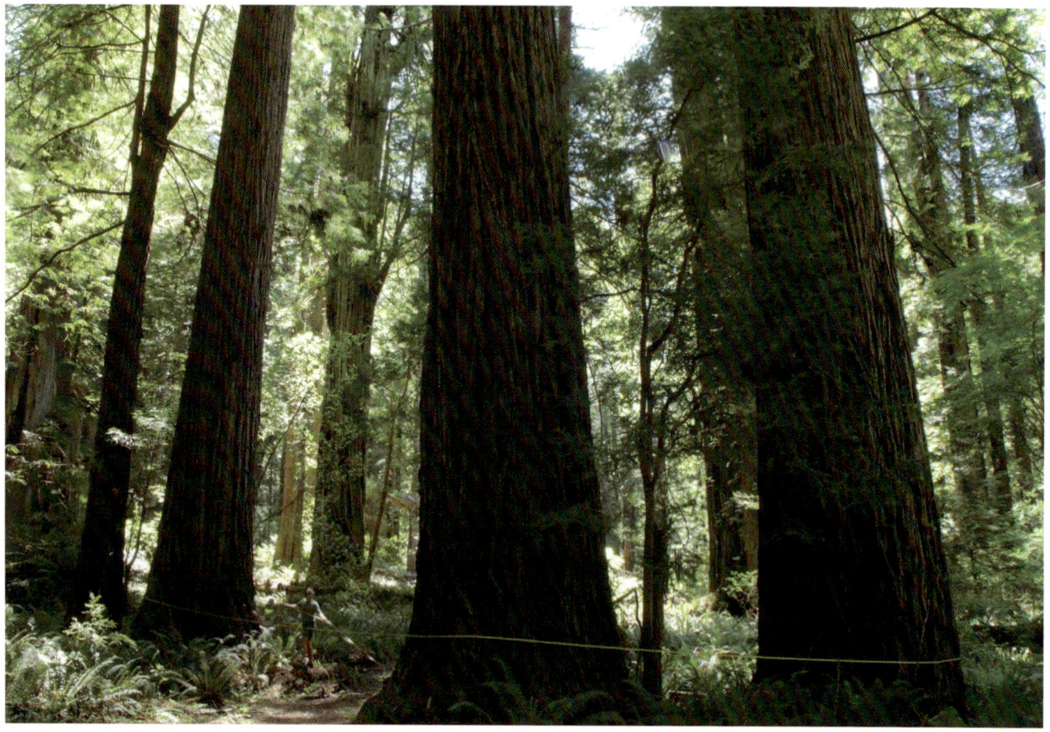

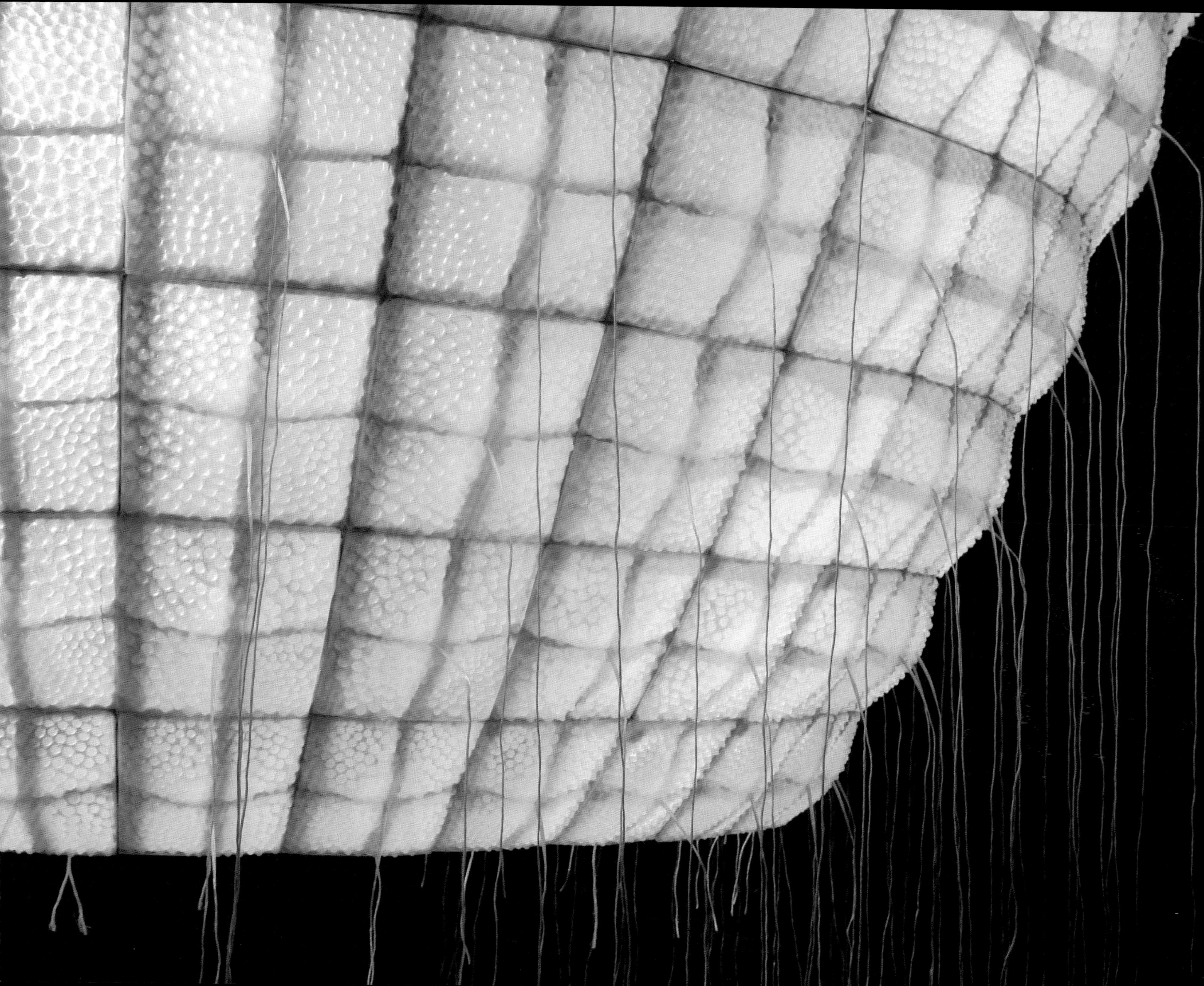

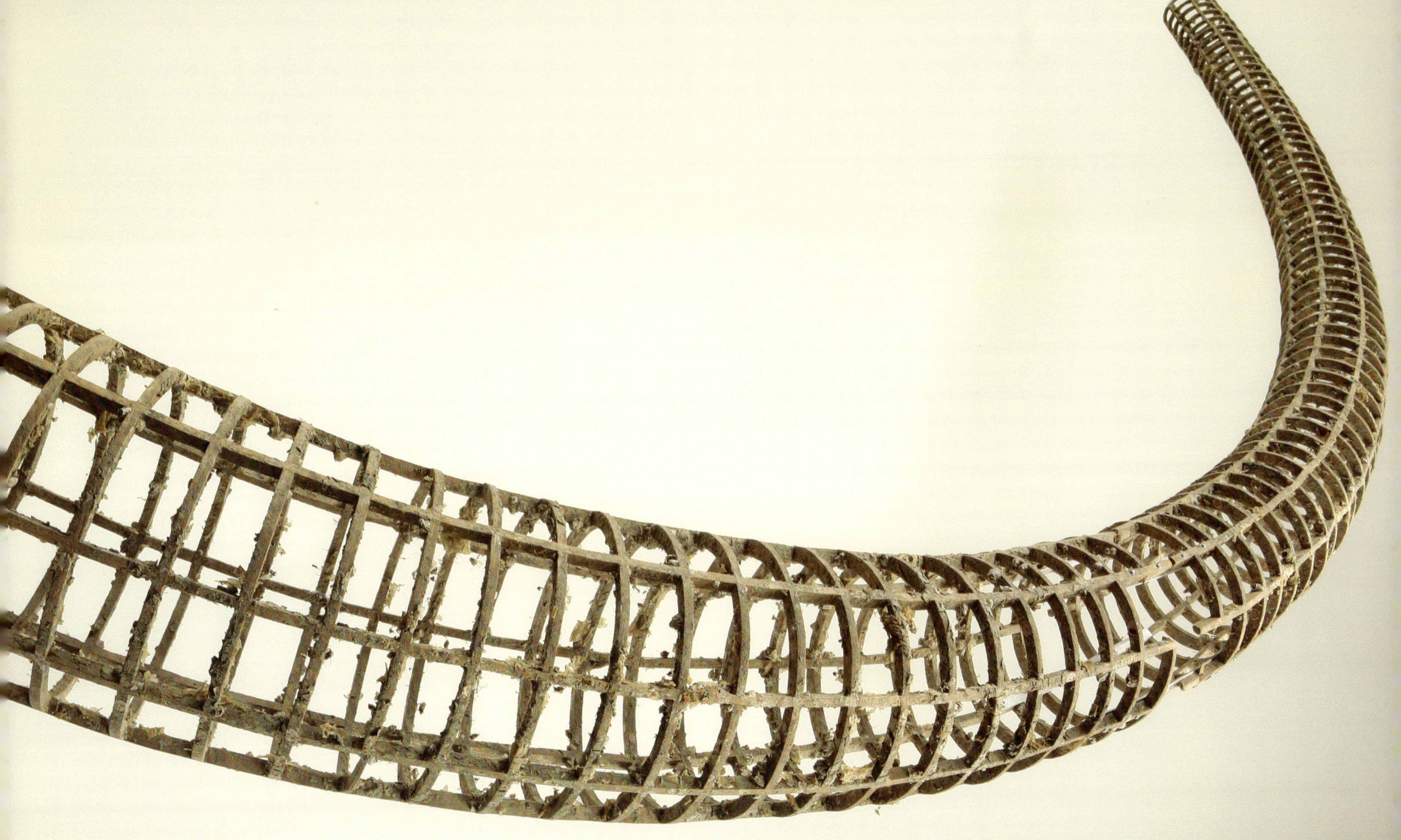

FOREWORD & ACKNOWLEDGMENTS

MICHAEL W. MONROE, DIRECTOR AND CHIEF CURATOR

John Grade: Disintegration, Sculpture Through Landscape is one of a series of exhibitions and monographs published by Bellevue Arts Museum featuring leading Pacific Northwest figures in the area of contemporary sculpture and mixed-media art. The series was initiated when the Museum reopened in June of 2005 as a strategy chosen to pay tribute to the richness and vibrancy of the work being created by some of the area's finest artists, while also honoring and strengthening the Museum's unique mission in the region.

This exhibition and its accompanying catalogue document a pivotal point in this Seattle-based artist's practice and together stand as a tangible visual and written record of his accomplishment. They are a testimony to John Grade's vision, which will remain long after the physical presence of the exhibition concludes. We are particularly honored and pleased to have played a critical role at this juncture in his artistic life.

We are deeply appreciative of John Grade's patience, cooperation, and thoughtful responses to an abundance of demands throughout the planning of the exhibition and catalogue. His insightfulness and guidance have been invaluable and are evidenced throughout. We wish to extend our heartfelt thanks to Driek and Michael Zirinsky and to the Tacoma Art Museum, whose support is evidenced by their willingness to loan works from their collections, thus revealing their broad and deep respect for the artist.

We are especially thankful for the generous support of the Institute for Museum and Library Services, the City of Bellevue, 4Culture, the City of Seattle's Office of Arts and Cultural Affairs, Artist Trust, Pollock-Krasner Foundation, Louis Comfort Tiffany Foundation, U.S. National Park Service, MacDowell Colony, the Espy Foundation, and Davidson Galleries, Seattle. Without their cooperation and generosity this exhibition and publication would not have been possible.

Bellevue Arts Museum curator Stefano Catalani is owed a special debt of gratitude for the curatorial skills he brings to Grade's work through the selection of works, his essay, and the presentation of the sculptures. We also thank Christopher Schnoor for his perceptive essay on this artist's work. Phil Kovacevich created the elegant catalogue; editorial review was provided by Sigrid Asmus. I also extend my sincerest appreciation and thanks to Bellevue Arts Museum's Board of Trustees, staff, docents, guilds, and volunteers for their ongoing support, enthusiasm, and trust in the Museum's mission.

Without question, we owe our greatest thanks to John Grade for creating these remarkable works, which help to define and redefine both the history of contemporary sculpture and the importance of site-specific installations in the Pacific Northwest. It is our hope that through these efforts new audiences will discover and interact with these provocative and stunning sculptures, while those who may already be familiar with his earlier work will gain fresh insights.

COLLECTOR (detail)
2007
Wood
8 x 72 x 78 in.

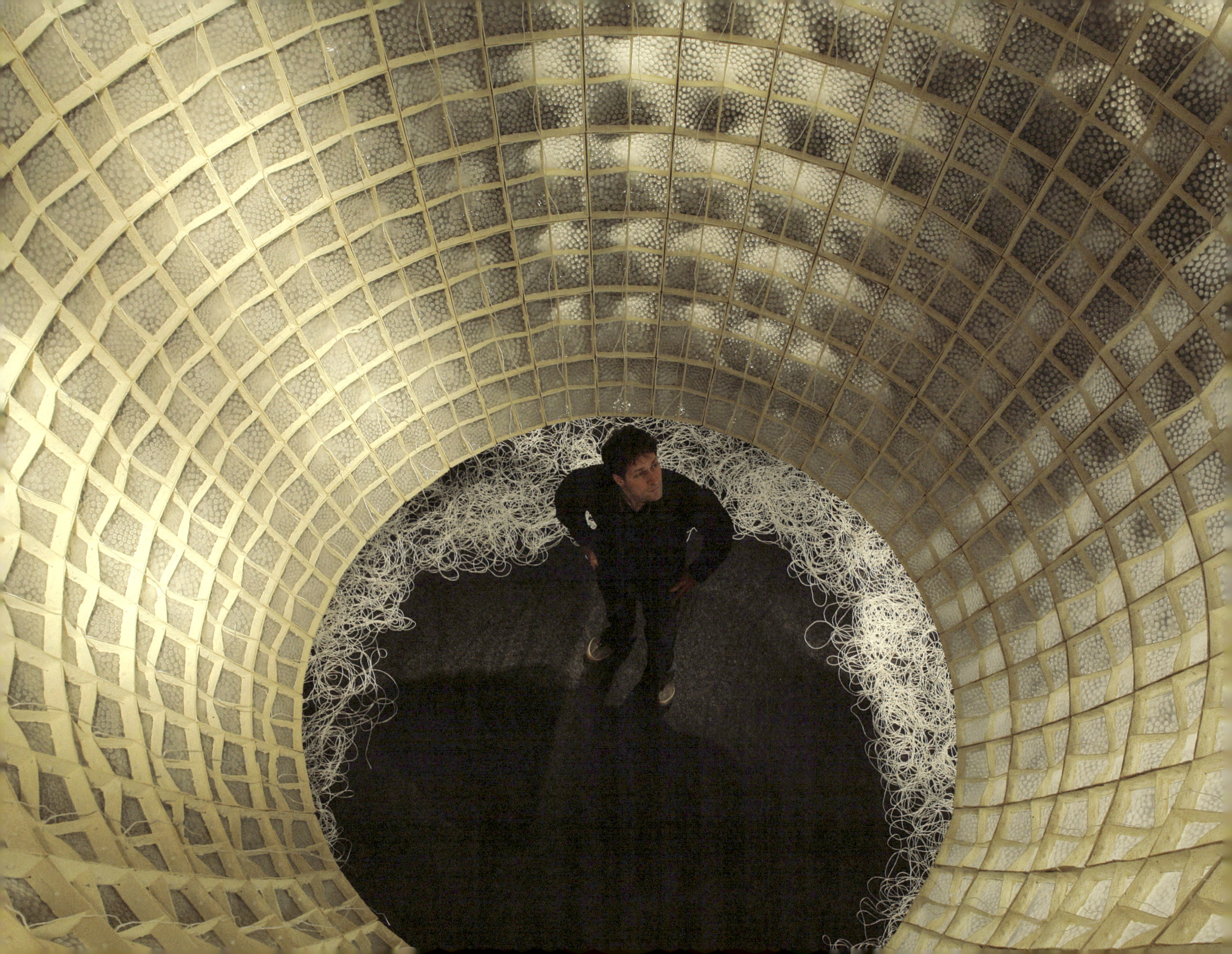

THE NATURAL COURSE OF THINGS

BY STEFANO CATALANI, CURATOR

> We are surrounded with things which we have not made and which have a life and structure different from our own: trees, flowers, grasses, rivers, hills, clouds. For centuries they have inspired us with curiosity and awe. They have been objects of delight. We have recreated them in our imaginations to reflect our moods. And we have come to think of them as contributing to an idea which we have called nature.
>
> —KENNETH CLARK[1]

WRITING ON THE ART OF LANDSCAPE PAINTING in the opening words of his *Landscape Into Art*, Kenneth Clark introduces us to the long-established tradition of nature in art as an idea—a recreation of the imagination—and the nature of art as a place for the projection of our moods, imaginings, emotions. By retracing the centuries-long transformation of the complexity of natural forces into the unity of an idea, Clark's concise first paragraph puts forward for consideration the way that nature, in art, has been invested with its role as the emotional and existential mirror of our lives. Once the natural world is tamed through the agency of light and color, or material and plastic values, we look at its representations—or rather presentations—as reflections of our hopes and expectations, fears and capitulations: we look to see ourselves.

This anthropomorphic vision of nature in art is an expression of the human pattern that relishes the power of metaphor to bestow meaning upon the apparent—and frighteningly incommensurable—chaos of nature. We *tend* to interpret a representation of nature as charged with a message pregnant with meaning for us. But how much of this presumed interpretation pertains to the physical objects we call art? Every time we look at a work of art we interpose our own specific ability to read the object. In other words, the cultural context and systems of beliefs we are part of cannot avoid meeting the pool of visual images, symbols, and modes of representation the artist used in creating the artwork in order to make it legible. Where does what I would like to call the image-object—with its attestations both of literal information (light, color, weight, material, form), and its metaphoric dimensions, if any—end? And where do the viewer's interpretations, with their own need to interiorize the work of art by projecting themselves inside the space of the artwork, begin? Moreover, once these two systems of information meet, which one controls and arbitrates the attribution of meaning? "All art is to some degree symbolic and recognition depends on certain long accepted formulae,"[2] writes Clark. These formulae are the conventions that regulate the attribution of meaning and the interpretation and utilization of the work of art, both in the private domain and in the sociocultural sphere. But while the deduction of the regulating formulae of the past

The artist inside *Meridian*

is the subject matter of iconographic studies, what happens with contemporary artists? The conventions that support and regulate the apprehension of the work of art should still be a common cultural currency. Yet the projection of the viewer's moods and emotions toward and into the art also remains. Can the artist make an object, with its unique set of physical signs and symbolic references, that forces the viewer to see it on its own terms? Or an image-object that minimizes the projections of the viewer?

John Grade: Disintegration, Sculpture through Landscape at Bellevue Arts Museum may offer one answer to this question. The exhibition begins exactly where the 2004 Boise Art Museum survey of Grade's work concluded. In the catalogue that accompanied that exhibition, critic Matthew Kangas predicted the oncoming change of direction in the Seattle-based artist's sculpture: "The works collected in Boise comprise a survey of 'early Grade'—sculptures inspired by long sojourns on five continents (Asia, Europe, Africa, North and South America)—because what will come later for Grade is bound to be of comparable interest, but it is unclear whether it will remain as closely tied to his poetics of place."[3] Grade was then thirty-four, and once the exhibition was over clearly felt he wanted to change what he did. "I was tired of people projecting themselves into my work—using it as a metaphor for what they thought."[4] When asked to expound upon a statement that seemed veiled with hubris, Grade explained, "There was this feeling of artifice. I came to realize that people were looking at my sculptures and not seeing them for the literal objects that they are. I realized people were not reading the objects on their terms!"[5] In his drive toward greater clarity for his work, Grade set out to search for new modes of making art that would help him redefine, or define in a more controlled way,

the relationship between the viewer and the artistic object. These modes would have to involve the construction of the physical and symbolic dimension of the objects themselves, while at the same time not hindering his ability to carry through his dominating idea of the romantic relationship between man and nature, and in fact would have to enrich and expand it. At first, the answer to his concerns came, with *Cleave*, from the embrace of a larger scale. Then, as with the more recent pieces *Fold*, *Host*, *Collector*, and *Meridian*, it came through employing nature as a tool in the artist's hands, and—as a surprising result of this decision—by largely releasing the new pieces from the force of his control.

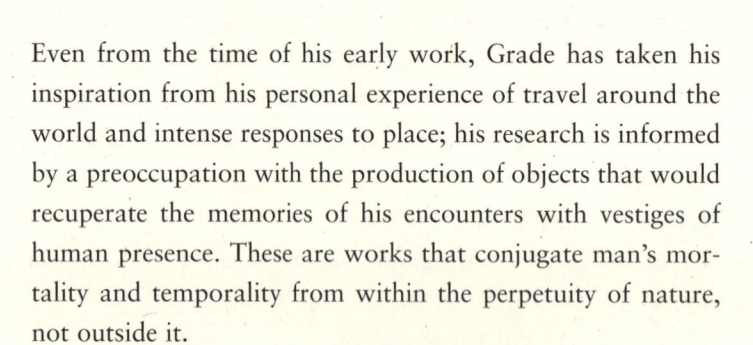

Even from the time of his early work, Grade has taken his inspiration from his personal experience of travel around the world and intense responses to place; his research is informed by a preoccupation with the production of objects that would recuperate the memories of his encounters with vestiges of human presence. These are works that conjugate man's mortality and temporality from within the perpetuity of nature, not outside it.

Works such as *Paired Cicatrice*, *Cuffs*, *Rift*, *Jaw*, *Costa*, *Greave*, *Greave Inside*, and *Hands* all call the human body directly into question by proxy, either through the parts referred to in their titles or their physical form. Indeed they speak of a dismembered and fragmented body, like the mutilated torsos, arms, and heads excavated from ancient sites. With the illusion of loss of completeness they stage, these pieces engulf the viewer with a sense of archaeological epiphany.

Other sculptures, such as *Tower Sillustani* (p. 54), *Tower Amantani*, *Burial Seed*, and *Confessional*, are informed by

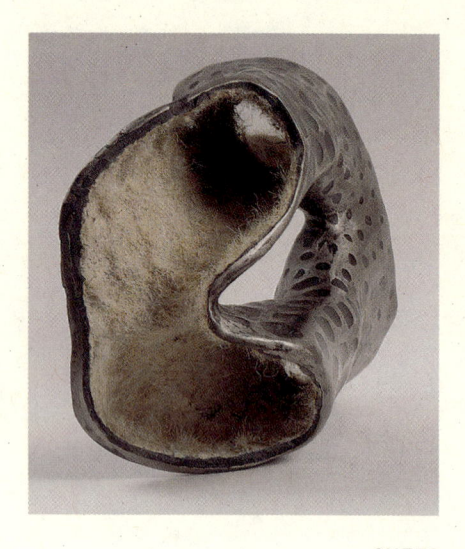

CUFFS
2003
Cast iron, resin, and fur
8 x 9 x 4 in.

(left)
RIFT
2003
Resin and wood
28 x 11 x 7 in.

(right)
HIDE
2002
Wood and resin
64 x 26 x 14 in.

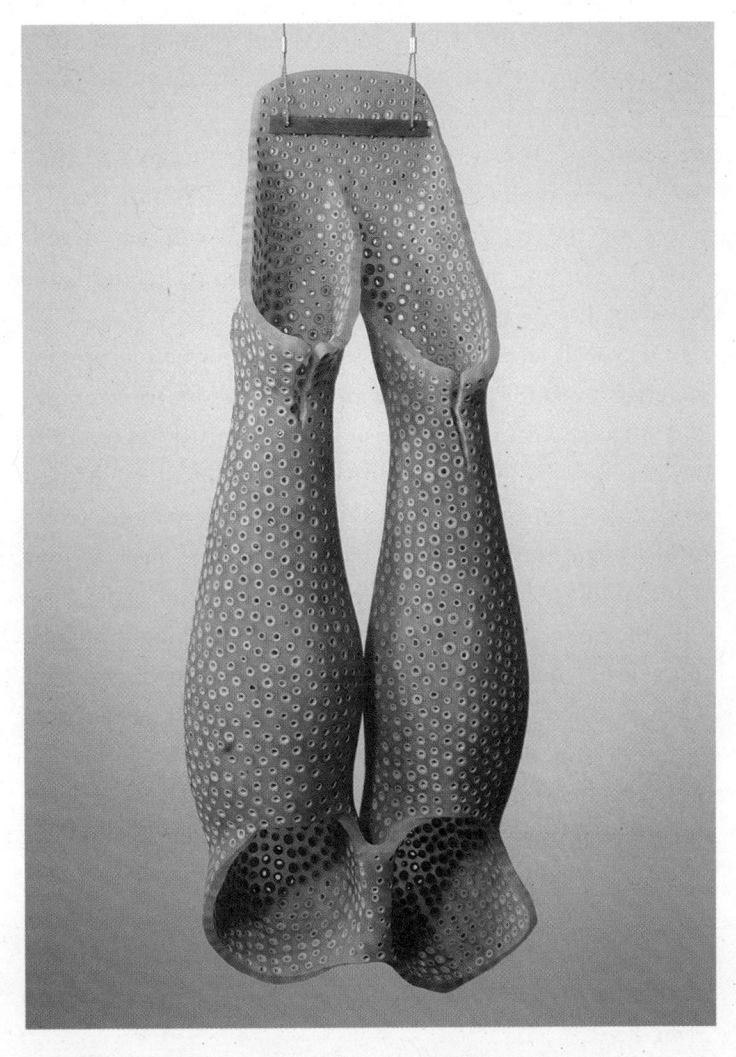

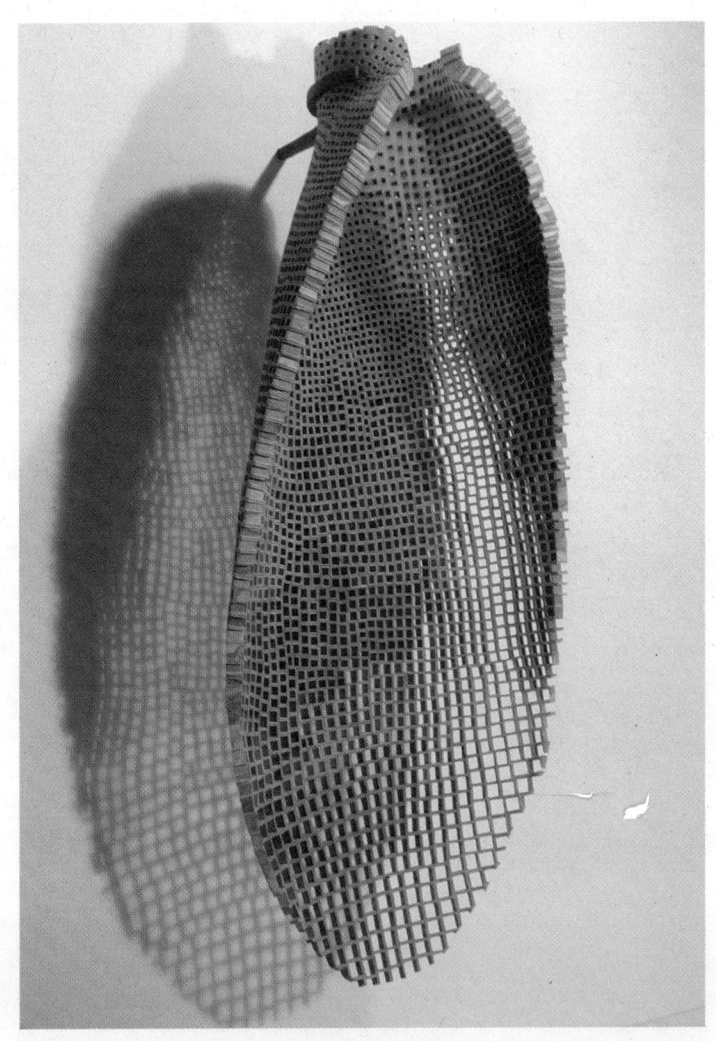

mortality. *Confessional* is a somber coffin-reliquary of wooden latticework. Its three sections open up to reveal a fragile, translucent, hollow cylindrical form—and some sort of biological sample resting inside. *Tower Sillustani* and *Tower Amantani* are five-foot-high structures inspired by the ruins of pre-Inca Peruvian funerary towers. In the intention of the artist, they celebrate, through the shadows they cast, the memory of the light of the Peruvian landscape Grade experienced and associated with mortality.

Other "early Grade" works—*Shoal (Bone Shoal Sonance)*, *Swell*, *Hide*, and many of the pencil drawings—play on the resemblance between man-made buildings and structures found in nature. Through the repetition of a cellular pattern, and whether square or circular, they can call to mind the footprints of urban dwellings, the cells of a honeycomb, clusters of marine life forms, or tissues on a Petri dish . . .

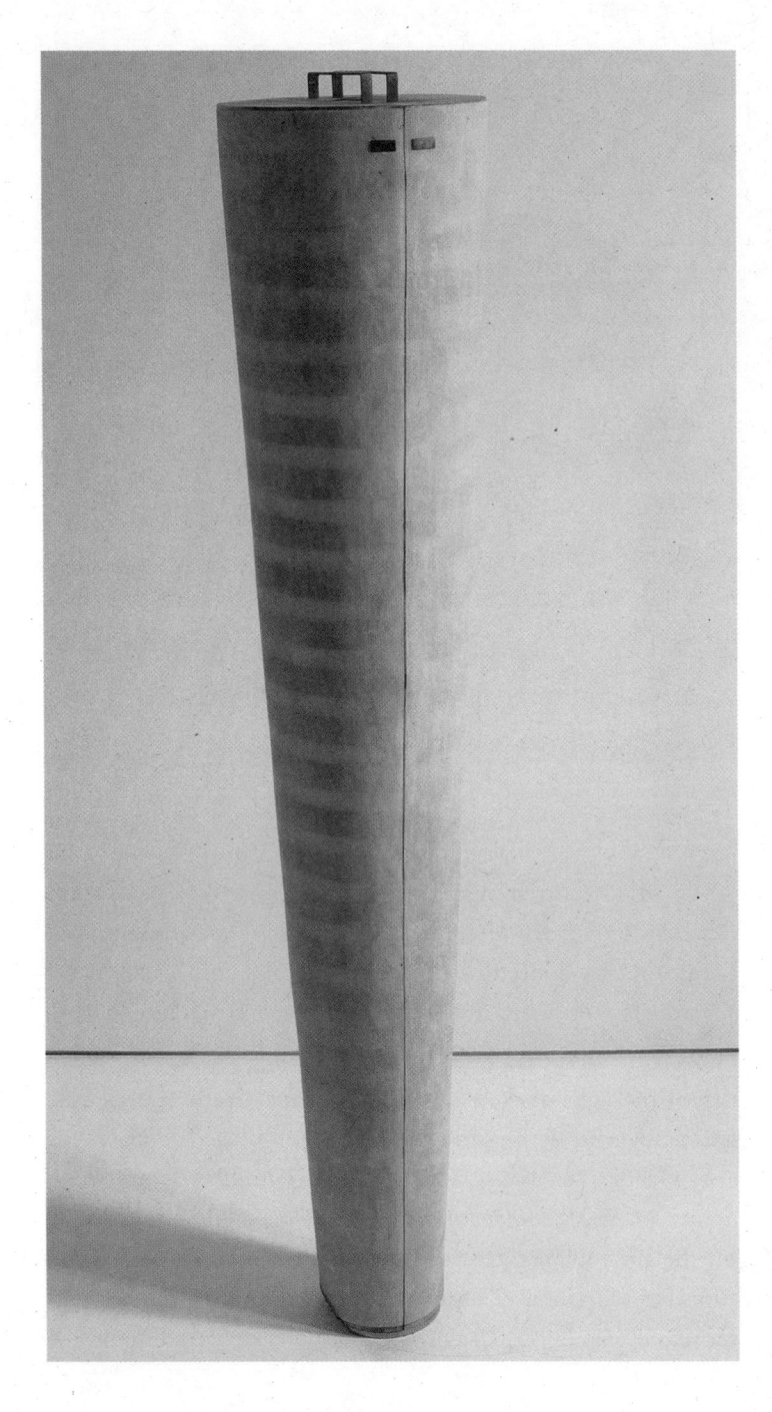

As one looks back at the earlier works from today's perspective, Grade's artistic focus can be recognized as a dialectic of traces of the human creative presence scattered across, unearthed from, and ultimately again absorbed into and becoming part of nature.

Through laborious processes of transformation of basic materials (wood, lead, leather, paper, and resin, for example) and intensive treatment of the surfaces, the artist has found an intrinsic way to incorporate psychological qualities in these works: they appear enshrouded in an aura of remote, undisturbed being, suspended like memories. It has been written that their practical purpose is unclear and that the artist "toys with the notion of usefulness rather than invoking particular functions."[6] But isn't this precisely the impression we have when we come across an artifact made in the past or by another culture, and whose use, now unclear, leaves us perplexed? We *know* that it was made for some purpose but we lack the essential information that might fully disclose its meaning. We might thus venture to say that Kangas's reaction is a consequence of the early works' aspiration to achieve an aura of artifact-vestiges, remnants of the expression of skill and imagination that has historically marked—and still marks—man's *being-here*.

Grade's fascination with the anthropological nature of these artifacts has moved him to reenact the feeling of discovering, handling, and trying to comprehend them; thus his sculptures are often mechanisms created of parts and hinges that open, interlock, and couple with no certain function except perhaps to reveal the mechanism itself (see *Carapace with Cuffs*, p. 56).

(above and left)
TOWER SILLUSTANI
1999
Resin, wood, steel, and lead
60 x 11 x 11 in.

BETWEEN TURF FACE AND
DEMESNE WALL
2005
Charcoal on paper
46 x 104 in.

There is also a dual temporal valence of the artifact as it exerts its attraction on the landscape of the artist's mind. As a factual, cultural expression of man's *being there*, the artifact acquires and reflects, by extension, the dimensions of the temporality as well as the finitude of life; at the same time, the artifact is invested by the possibility—or rather the promise—that it can survive its creator. In this sense, Grade's sculptures embody a mnemonic function, allowing us to see them as devices that assist in a wider, archetypal remembering that encompasses more than just the artist. By articulating a language of impermanence, these unresolved objects bridge the distance that separates the artist's own memories of the places he visited and the people who left traces in those places. They thus join aspects of the inborn memory of our mortal dimension, the anticipation of our death, and the concern for the traces we will leave behind, embraced, as they must be, by the landscape they will become part of. The visual assonances between natural and man-made structures in works such as *Shoal (Bone Shoal Sonance)*, *Swell*, *Hide*, or many of the drawings, also stress the clouding of the distinctness of these traces within the landscape that consumes and preserves them.

The works featured in *John Grade: Disintegration, Sculpture Through Landscape* continue to express the fascination of the artist for the dialectic of presence and absence, reflecting a broadening of the artist's vocabulary and marking a shift beyond the object-driven. Four of the five pieces in the exhibition, namely *Host*, *Fold*, *Meridian*, and *Collector*, are divested of the illusion the artist had employed to give substance to his romantic poetics of impermanence, and instead are invested with—and embody—a new dimension of reality. The duotoned title *Disintegration* reflects our intention to capture the spirit of Grade's new direction. Here, the large sculptural objects—and the accompanying photographs of the pieces in different locations—explore sculpture as a presence both created and destroyed through landscape. From the oyster fields of Willapa Bay, in Washington State, to the deserts and slot canyons of the Southwest, Grade's constructions are—and were, and will be—placed in natural settings, and in this process are themselves informed and altered by their interaction with nature. The artist's vision of integration with the natural environment also includes an ensuing disintegration, in which both the voluptuous and the tragic, the architectural and the organic relationships between art as the handmade and nature—the *things which we have not made*—takes on an interesting tenuousness.

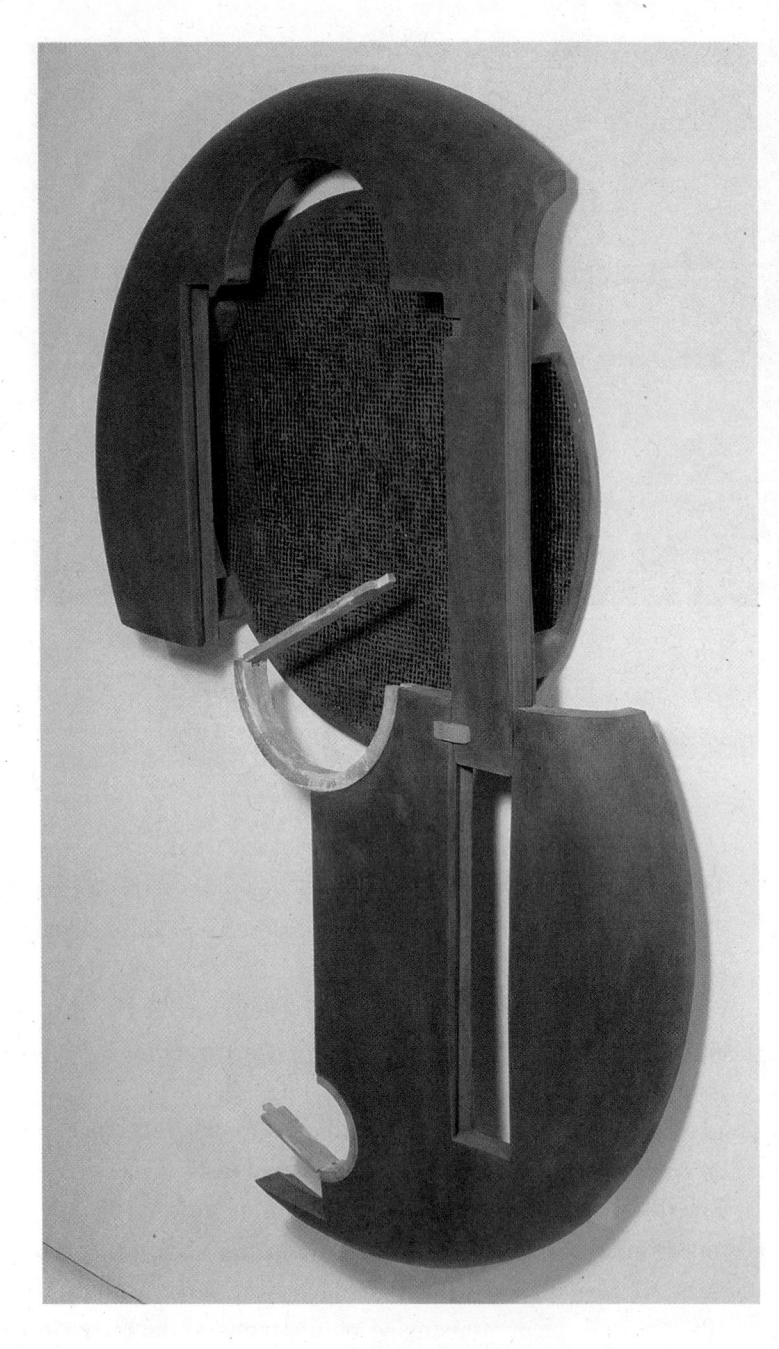

Grade exhibits his projects at different stages of development—rudimentary, full-grown, encrusted, consumed, collapsed, and absorbed by the earth below—and the revolutionary aspect of this strategy is that no single stage could possibly be considered the most complete or final. The larger scale of these pieces reveals a new way that nature, and specifically its vastness—may be embraced. At the same time, the play between the artist's desire to control their future embodiment and his renunciation of a fully controlled gestation establishes a new vantage point from which we must regard these objects. In the presence of these pieces and installations the viewer is left to unravel the events of the journey thus far and to marvel at the unfolding possibilities. It would be a mistake to interpret the photographs accompanying the exhibition as a mere narrative support; their presence here—and in a more substantial way in this catalogue—is intended to help the viewer address the real temporal dimension of these works. Presented in scattered sequences, the photographs are snapshots of the lives of these objects thus far.

(above and left)
CARAPACE WITH CUFFS
2000
Slate, steel, wood, and resin
39 x 39 x 7 in.

Cleave is the first work the artist created while in the process of shifting the center of gravity of his new work from the viewer-object relationship to the object itself, a central change in the apprehension of the work. In the statement accompanying the exhibition *Cleave* at Davidson Galleries in Seattle, Grade acknowledges that

> *Cleave* represents a transition within my interest in addressing landscape. Previously I have explored and made work in response to landscapes that carry culturally assigned significance pertaining to how people die. Some of these sites have been clearly defined by architecture, like burial structures or cemeteries. Other sites have had little or no current discernible human imprint, but are sites that hold historical significance. The shift in this new body of work lies in an exploration of landscapes that fall within the idea of wilderness. Evidence of human alteration exists in these "wild" landscapes, but it is not the primary aspect of the sites that I aim to consider.[7]

The artist further elucidates the way he now wishes to "focus instead on the significance of water. These landscapes are cut open by the movement of water and defined through bursts, slow accumulation, and in frozen cleaving."[8] While the theme of water may have been *Cleave*'s first inspiration, from a formal standpoint the shift in scale is the first element that leads us to feel that a change is occurring in the artist's approach to his art. As the artist notes, his attention is now focused on the *nature* term of the equation rather than on the human presence *in* nature—whose features are both perceived and delivered through their scale.

In 2004 and 2005 the artist traveled extensively through the Escalante Plateau in Utah and the glacial fields of the Cascade Range, and on two occasions was compelled to face the physical possibility of his death. The first came during a training excursion on the south side of Mount Rainier when he fell into a crevasse. For a short time he was suspended on belay, but then his partners lost control of the situation and he began to descend until he was only able to stop the fall by planting the blades of the crampons of his boots in the walls of ice. With just fifteen to twenty feet of slack rope and the dark, unfathomable fissure below him, and only his own strength to rely on, the artist experienced the vertigo of the cathedral-blue ice chasm. On the other occasion, he and his wife were caught by a summer storm while committed to a sixteen-mile hike at the bottom of a slot canyon in southern Utah. As the gorge rapidly filled with the torrential downpour, they were aware that steep drop-offs ahead would require roping down and up, and knew they had no other choice than to spend the night atop a sand mound that barely broke the surface of the water, taking turns to sleep. *Cleave* conflates these experiences of vulnerability and excitement into a single massive illusion. With its seventeen-foot-long and eleven-foot-high walls, made of clear resin and grafted with goat hair, *Cleave* is a towering, arched, narrow passage whose exit cannot be seen as one enters.[9] As in several other pieces, light plays a paramount part in the experience of the work. Once inside, we are caught in a cyclical series of transitions—from a deep, translucent, ice-blue illumination to a duller, drier, sandstone-brown. The artist notes, "Shifting light is the primary means of orienting a viewer's attention between these two experiential outlooks."[10] As we make our way through, *Cleave* stages another subtle psychological shift as the horizontal split that traverses the whole length of the passage imperceptibly increases, gradually instilling a sense of discomfort; are we slowly moving "deeper" or are we "under," *as if* submerged? Interred?

Cleave stands as a device of sensory and psychological overload. Every element here works to elicit feelings of cautiousness and intrigue: the towering walls, like those in Richard Serra's steel spirals, trigger a sense of vulnerability and awe; the bend of the narrow passage precludes a sense of any certain escape; the slowly shifting lights and colors snag the viewer's curiosity and slow down his or her pace; and the surreal, inexplicable goat fur puzzles us with its pungent smell.

Here, as in earlier works, light is associated with a landscape of mortality. And yet it is in the intuitive choice to bend the passage, hiding from sight its finite dimension, that Grade touches upon the incommensurability of nature and achieves a poetic high. When I first entered *Cleave* I could not avoid the association with death and the words of poet Fernando Pessoa: "La morte è la curva della strada / morire è solo non essere visto": Death is the bend of the road / to die is only not to be seen.[11]

Cleave is a transitional piece; it is a bend that turns in a new direction yet it remains strongly tied to the world of *image illusions* of the "early Grade." Those pieces were born having their adult, final appearance when they emerged from the artist's hands. They were, are, and will be indefinitely suspended in this static stage unless some unexpected incident damages or destroys them. Theirs is the simulation of a fragmented, finite, and transient reality that mirrors the riddle of human existence. *Cleave*'s subject is still the body and our reflection upon its vulnerability, yet the sculpture nevertheless operates in the domain of the creation of an illusionistic space,

CLEAVE (detail)
2006
Clay, goat fur, resin, and video projection
156 x 45 x 288 in;
interior passage approximately
123 x 26 x 184 in.

of an "as if." The object neither confronts the viewer with a real threat, nor presents reality as found in nature. Yet *Cleave* invites the viewer to absorb the artist's experiences of vulnerability through its translucent, nonporous walls, and in so doing requests the viewer's participation—by means of his or her own projections—in the spectacle that it stages. In other words, the object is now both literally and metaphorically open-ended.

Fold, *Collector*, *Host*, and *Meridian* articulate the full extent of Grade's intent to minimize the projection of the viewer's "self" onto the artwork, and instead to impel viewers to relate to them on their own terms. However, because Chris Schnoor so ably recounts the history of these four pieces in his essay in this catalogue, I will analyze only two of them here in order to bring out and focus on the artistic solutions Grade's new direction presents.

Composed of two curved, tusk-shaped, cagelike, wood structures that when connected create a circle about six and a half feet in diameter, *Collector* made its debut in a Seattle gallery mounted on the wall, pristine and fresh from the studio. This early display of the work as an newly built structure gives that moment the symbolic value of a birth. As such, its continuing appearance is relevant to the construction of its story, and part of the account of past events in its life, since those visitors to the Bellevue exhibition who may first have seen the piece in Seattle will now experience a different object, one now two years older.

Collector's life was affected by having been placed within the landscape. For a year, it was left below the waters of Willapa Bay on the Pacific coast, to be encrusted by oysters, seaweed, and other marine life forms. Later it was mounted on the hood of a pickup truck and moved to Utah to be left at the bottom of a slot canyon where scouring waters would be allowed to take their toll. Shaped to fit into a sinuous crack in the rock of a particular canyon, however, *Collector* could not be set in place when the artist found prior rains had clogged the site with debris and tree branches. And so it was left up on the Plateau—held by straps and suspended in a wooden frame. *Collector* collected on its "skin" the traces of every day it spent in the landscapes it was placed within, from the most evident crustacean incrustations—later picked at by birds—to the most elusive gathering of smashed insects on the highway trip.

Meridian is a large-scale sculpture built in hundreds of independent sections and designed to both collapse and evolve while sited within two contrasting landscapes. As the artist describes it, *Meridian* is

cast in a composite of rubber, fabric, and lightweight rigid foam. Assembled for the first time in Bellevue, it will be sited next in Arizona at the mouth of a slot canyon, spanning a chasm like a series of delicate ring-like bridges. Just prior to being sited in the desert, I will coat the sculpture with several thin layers of cellulose and casein.

On the rim, the cables threaded within *Meridian* will extend horizontally, staking the sculpture in place by anchoring it to heavy vessels full of water. Released from the weight of these vessels as the water evaporates, the interconnected rings will start folding in upon themselves like collapsing marionettes. The individual transparent segments will tumble down fifty feet into the narrow fissure, arrested in mid fall and prevented from hitting the canyon floor by the umbilical-like cord anchored to the center of each part.

Chosen for its periodic thermal updrafts, the site will funnel wind upward, lifting and entangling the parts, culminating in one condensed monolithic form. The sculpture will then be removed intact and moved to a second site, an old growth coastal redwood forest in California, where it will be suspended one hundred feet up into the tree canopy.

Here, it will gradually begin to transform. The coastal mist, fog, and regular rain will turn the dry, thin skins of cellulose and casein into a gelatinous glue. The pitted texture of the cast foam elements will attract and retain falling organic matter that will mix with the moist cellulose and casein and gradually harden, fixing *Meridian* into a new configuration reflective of the canopy.[12]

Grade's earlier works were created to reflect the artist's experiences of cultural and natural landscapes, and they rely on a re-creation of the effects of the forces shaping those very landscapes. Their static and final completeness expresses a sense of control.

By contrast, *Fold*, *Collector*, *Host*, and *Meridian* exist with and within nature: they change, move, rise, and collapse in response to being directly affected by the forces of nature itself. Each of the pieces is a real result—not an *as if* one—of the agencies of weather and countless other elements of the natural environment, some foreseeable, some unpredictable. They are made by the landscape as much as by the artist. In their powerful emotional presence, these works rely upon an orchestrated tension that is put in place between an initial craftsmanship that attempts to assert control over future possible outcomes, and the full abandonment of artistic control. Any predictable conclusion of their existence is denied. As the shaping forces that bestow formal values upon and inform the final artistic result, natural processes seize Grade's sculptures while charging them with a new and evocative metaphor of human existence. The illusion of the early works has been dispelled, and we are left with the real and uncertain opaqueness of life.

In abandoning an illusionistic space where memories and projections are conflated, the artist's poetics of impermanence and romantic longing for the traces that remain—of one, one hundred, or a hundred thousand lives—have found a new voice. Through working within nature and with time, *Fold*, *Collector*, *Host*, and *Meridian* reduce the impacts of natural forces to mere tools—or rather to something like an automaton, a device that performs a function according to a predetermined set of coded instructions. Nevertheless, if this is a device, the artist cannot fully control the forces operating it, for it must respond not only to predicted circumstances but also to aleatory factors that might easily skew the outcome in ways the artist had not planned. *Fold* and *Meridian* are about to be deployed into the landscape, carrying an embedded "genetic code" of responses to certain expected outside stimuli for which the artist has carefully designed them. But once in the landscape anything could happen. They could change in time as per Grade's expectations, but something could also go "wrong," and a piece might be completely destroyed; it's even possible that the only trace left to testify to its existence may be the images in this publication. I purposefully have placed "wrong" in quotation marks to draw attention to the consideration that there can be no wrong in nature: wrong, with the meaning of not correct or true, is not a category in nature.

Fold, *Meridian*, *Host*, and *Collector* rely on the passage of time to acquire their meaning. These are objects that measure—by collapsing, slowly disappearing, or simply changing—the reality of the inexorable passing of time. They will exist and survive in spite of accidents, difficult or adverse circumstances, and mere chance until the day they will no longer exist. They are made by and *of* time: the time that remains between the now and their certain but completely undetermined obliteration. Only their sturdier, almost negligible, traces might remain, like fragments of a skull may reappear hundreds of thousands of years after the body was consumed. In Heideggerian terms, with their temporal dimension *Fold*, *Meridian*, *Host*, and *Collector* put us in a "mood" or "feeling" that attunes us with our impermanence. These objects' real, material disintegration (as shown by the pieces themselves, and as inferred through the photographs) projects onto us the finitude of our being-here, of our being-in-the-world, and of the undetermined certainty—whose moment can't be known—of our death, our *no-more*, which is still a *not-yet*. Just as with the earlier Grade works, each of the new pieces already is, and will be, a remnant, a vestige—or, paradoxically, a *natural* artifact. There is no simulation, no illusion in these objects. Like living creatures they are survivors within the passage of time: what we see, what we experience, is the trace of the past they had. A history of scars and scoured surfaces, marks and missing parts for *Host* and *Collector*, a brand-new skeleton and skin for *Meridian* and *Fold*. What they are given for the future is time, although no one knows how much more.

In his efforts to create objects that would not merely act as occasions for viewers to project their individual responses but instead retain an opacity that requires that one apprehend the object on its terms, the artist has progressively removed himself from the making of the artwork. His craft is now circumscribed by the design and construction of the original structures, his actions limited to moving and positioning them. In doing so Grade has not lost sight of his ideas, but he has developed a new vocabulary. Once the objects are modified by natural causes—whether the currents of the bay, wind and rain, the melting ice of a glacier, or the oysters and the barnacles and the seaweeds, the birds, insects, and termites—their trajectory has changed. They are now, step after step, increasingly removed from the possibility of being *interpreted* as a map of the private and personal emotions of the artist in which viewers attempt to mirror their personal worlds. We are left instead to deal with natural and universal causes and effects that, once internalized, cannot help but reveal the vulnerability and finitude of life. These are objects that speak of the process of their creation rather than of their creator.

The place for Grade's new sculptures is in nature, across and through the landscape. Meanwhile, the placement of these four most recent works in the museum's galleries exposes the limitations of museum space as an artificial, premeditated, and unnatural setting for the sculptures. In their setting here, one feels these pieces—with their osmotic and entropic relationship with nature, their belonging hitherto and afterward to nature and its field of inexorable forces—reveal the inherent fragility of the museum gallery. In their changed role, the galleries appear as a suspensive (as in suspended animation), celebratory, and therefore inappropriate context, the site of a sort of traveling sideshow where the main attraction is on view only while the circus is in town. Within the asphyxiating frame of an architectural space, John Grade's newest work clarifies the inadequacy of the museum setting and the limitations it can have as a place of mummified experiences for the audience. *Fold*, *Collector*, *Host*, and *Meridian* are works made to breathe in the air and water that literally gnaw them away. Their presence could also appear to transform the museum into a museum of natural history where specimens are preserved in formaldehyde and alcohol, with all their biometric data meticulously catalogued. Or perhaps, in a romantic vein, to an eighteenth-century cabinet of wonders and monstrosities, with these pieces as contemporary Leviathans. As curator, I could not help but think of the mummification the artist and I were staging as we proceeded to preserve these sculptures from their natural course of disintegration by essentially embalming and wrapping them in the cloth of the museum's authority and future pedigree. In a very genuine way the exhibition represents a hiatus in the natural course of things, at least for *Host* and *Collector*, which have already been deployed in nature. For *Fold* and *Meridian* it is more a matter of captivity that defers their introduction into the landscape. The *natural course of things* for these sculptures is not being on display in a museum. The humidity- and temperature-controlled galleries, and the measurement of footcandles of light exposure, are extraneous to their existence. Their place is out there, in the fiery-hot or flash-flooding slot canyons, in the temperate coastal redwood forest, or underground in the dry country of Nevada. They live where disintegration takes over.

It is only from this perspective, then, as we acknowledge the extraneousness of the museum experience to the life cycle of these sculptures—the *extraordinary* setting of a gallery—that we can infer their *ordinary* dimension: their being part of the normal, the expected course of nature. And so their presence here is truly how we celebrate these works, as we register and then nourish the recognition that these objects should not have been removed from the natural course of things—that they should not be here.

I want to extend my deepest thanks to the artist for his art and for his dedication to this project. It has been a pleasure to work with him and visit his studio in the International District in Seattle where *Meridian* and *Fold* took shape and the time flew by as the opening date of the exhibition approached. Their delivery—as with babies—was indeed accompanied by great expectations, inevitable labor, and the thrill of arrival.

I am grateful to Bellevue Arts Museum Executive Director Michael Monroe for his support and enthusiasm for this exhibition.

I offer many thanks to Christopher Schnoor, for his essay and his ability to respond to a tight deadline. Christopher's voice is authoritative and his detailed analysis of John's work is closely observed, accurate, and valid.

Last but not least I would like to express my heartfelt gratitude to Bellevue Arts Museum Head Preparator Vincent Warner and his crew for their outstanding skills, conscientiousness, and hard work in installing the five sculptures. Many thanks also go to Exhibitions Curator Nora Atkinson, Registrar Ester Fajzi, and all the staff of the curatorial department for their generous and unfailing dedication.

NOTES

[1] Kenneth Clark, *Landscape Into Art* (New York: HarperCollins, 1979), p. 1.

[2] Ibid., p. 3.

[3] Matthew Kangas, "John Grade: Excursions and Interventions," in *John Grade: Sculpture and Drawings* (Boise, ID: Boise Art Museum, 2004), p. 13.

[4] Frances DeVuono, *Seeps of Winter*, Suyama Space (Seattle, Washington, 2008).

[5] Interview with the artist, August 6, 2008.

[6] "Function and practical purpose, hallmarks of much contemporary craft art, are left undetermined in Grade; he toys with the notion of usefulness rather than invoking particular functions associated with traditional crafts media such as clay, glass, wood, textiles and metals." Matthew Kangas, "John Grade: Excursions and Interventions," p. 13.

[7] Artist's statement from the May 11–June 24, 2006, exhibition at Davidson Galleries, Seattle, Washington.

[8] Ibid.

[9] "The molds for the walls of the installation were built horizontally in the negative of the finished furry surface. This negative was a composite of wet clay and sheared goat hair (about 5000 pounds of them, when mixed together). Resin and fiberglass cloth were applied to this clay/goat-hair surface in many thin layers. Once the resin shell set and cured, the clay was gradually submerged and washed away with water, leaving roots of fur embedded within the clear resin surface. The goat hair mixed into the clay also served as a kind of binder that prevented the mixture from cracking and pulling apart as it dried." Artist's statement from the May 11–June 24, 2006 exhibition *Cleave* at Davidson Galleries, Seattle, Washington.

[10] Artist's statement, May 11–June 24, 2006 exhibition at Davidson Galleries.

[11] Fernando Pessoa, *Il Poeta è un Fingitore*, translated from the Portuguese by A. Tabucchi (Milano: Giangiacomo Feltrinelli Editore, 2004), p. 17. My translation from the Italian.

[12] Artist's email to the author, August 22, 2008.

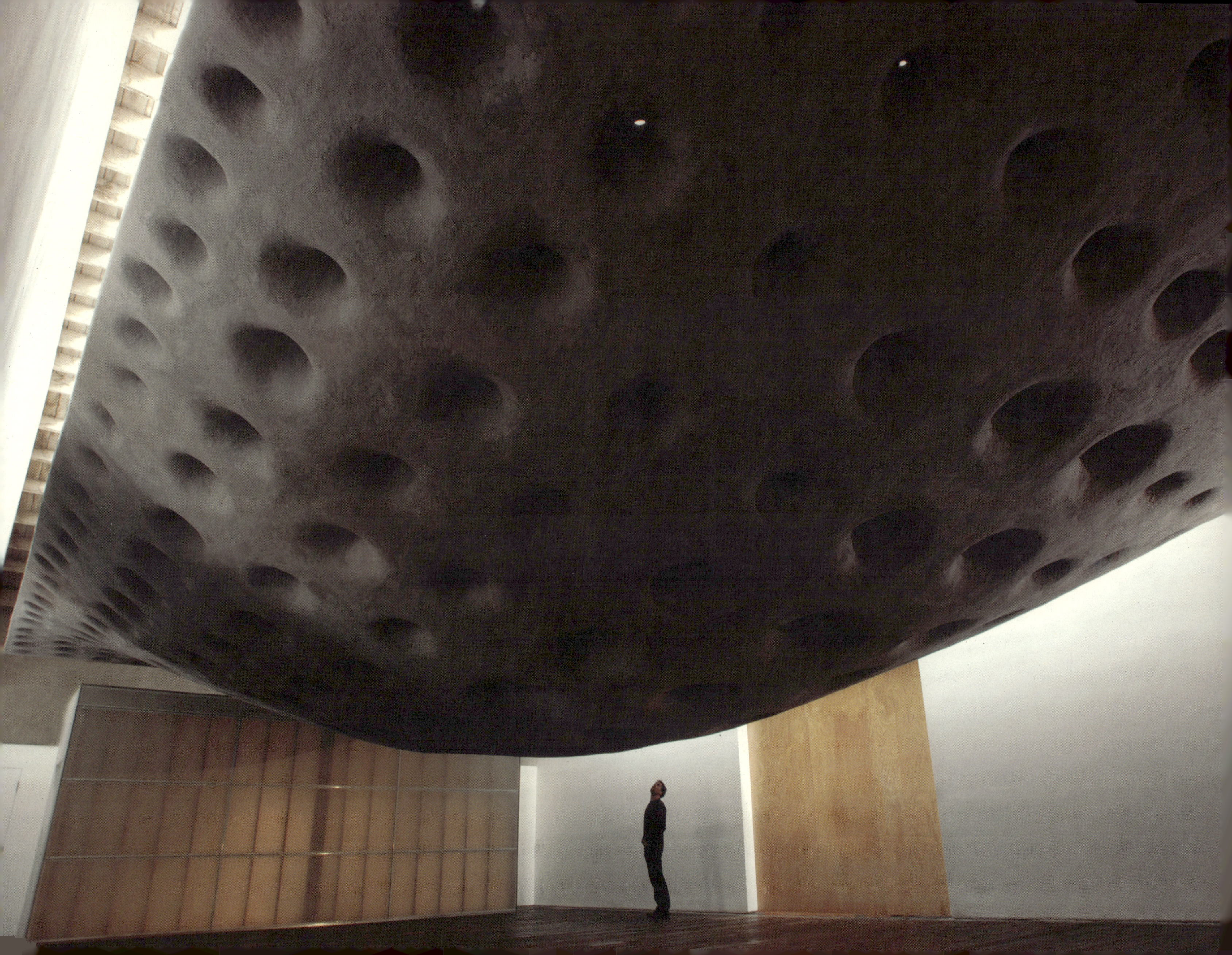

MULTIPLE LIVES The Itinerant Sculpture of John Grade

BY CHRISTOPHER SCHNOOR

> *Now the good life could be to cross a field*
> *And art a paradigm of earth new from the lathe*
> *Of ploughs.*
> —SEAMUS HEANEY, *Field Work*[1]

> *Before it can ever be a repose for the senses, landscape is the work of the mind.*
> —SIMON SCHAMA, *Landscape and Memory* [2]

FORTY YEARS AGO, in October 1968, the Dwan Gallery on New York's 57th Street heralded a new movement in art with an innovative group show of ten artists entitled *Earth Works*. The exhibition was a seminal event that included such works as Robert Morris's pile of dirt and industrial debris called *Earthwork*, and Robert Smithson's *A Nonsite, Franklin, New Jersey*, comprised of five trapezoidal bins filled with rocks, plus photographs and artifacts of projects by other artists sited in outdoor locations. It was revolutionary on two levels. First, although presented in a mainstream gallery-row space, the Dwan exhibition inherently subverted the relevance of such traditional venues, adding fuel to the "out of the box" dynamic that increasingly dominated contemporary art at the end of 1960s; and second, it took the concept of the radical potential of non-art materials and mediums to a new level, one that was not only anti-elitist but in many cases anti-form, while at the same time dovetailing with the emerging public awareness of environmental issues.

In the decades since, of course, what has become known as earth or land or environmental art has had a long list of notable practitioners including Robert Irwin, James Turrell, Richard Long, Alice Aycock, Andy Goldsworthy, and Patrick Dougherty, to name a few. Each, in their individual way, and often in remote wilderness settings, transformed the planet's most basic, mundane substances into a sculptural medium and created a new kind of art that can be described as "landscape as sculpture."

For Seattle-based artist John Grade, these labels fit rather uncomfortably. Unlike the earlier earth artists who chose permanent outdoor sites where their work was made and meant to be seen, the excursions Grade's sculptures make into the wild are private and temporary, part of the process but not the end destination. It is a testimony to the originality of his sculpture that it defies the shopworn categories of art criticism. In this, he can be almost as perverse as his predecessors at the Dwan Gallery, but it is perversity of a different sort. His is not

SEEPS OF WINTER
2008
Cast paper pulp, glassine, and fumed silica
120 x 600 x 360 in.

an anti-aesthetic bent on soiling the purity of "elitist" art, although Grade's new work also embraces entropy. Grade's contrariness is more subtle and has a teasing aspect to it that is best expressed in those pieces that play with our perceptions through ambiguous forms and suggestive associations, instilling an element of doubt that undermines their quasi-familiarity. It is also evident in his ability to make us feel slightly uncomfortable, as in the claustrophobic *Cleave* or the imposing mass hovering inches above our heads in the recent *Seeps of Winter*.

But this is not to say there are no precedents for Grade's approach to sculpture. As art critic Matthew Kangas has written, Grade's aesthetic is firmly rooted in that of Postminimalism, and in his emphasis on process, impermanence, and chance we see the markings of artists like Eva Hesse, Lynda Benglis, Bruce Nauman, and others. Richard Serra has set an important precedent as well, not only in his Postminimalist moment and early landscape pieces but also through the earthiness of his sculpture generally, the way it relates to the body and the passage of time, and in his return of the outdoor aesthetic to indoor venues. Gordon Matta-Clark, with his influential urban version of earth art, his proclivity for turning environments inside out, and his interest in issues of decay and renewal, can also be seen as a forerunner of Grade's endeavors.

Nor is Grade alone in his quest to broaden sculpture's horizons today. Among his contemporaries, Olafur Eliasson, who also uses landscape components in his art, shares Grade's focus on creating experiences rather than static representations. Critic Peter Schjeldahl's recent description of Eliasson as an artist whose "character suggests both the mental discipline of a scientist and the emotional responsibility of a poet,"[3] fits Grade perfectly. Grade has found inspiration, too, in the works of two contemporary British artists, Turner Prize–winner Simon Starling, and Darren Almond, both of whom interact with landscape through sculptural projects that incorporate ideas about nature and technology, time, geography, and space. Yet Grade is clearly on his own track, approaching his art with a single-mindedness that tunes out distracting art-world buzz about what's hot and what's not.

Four years ago, at the age of thirty-four, Grade was at a crossroads in his art. His exhibit of forty sculptures and drawings at the Boise Art Museum in 2004 surveyed a body of work completed over six years, and an intellectual process going back well before that. It was his first solo museum exhibition but also marked the end of an important first phase in his career as a sculptor. Although many of the concepts and sensibilities he developed in this period would continue to inform his art, Grade's restless mind was already headed in new directions, conceiving projects on a grander scale. A mere four years later, *Disintegration: Sculpture Through Landscape*

SEEPS OF WINTER (view from above)
2008
Cast paper pulp, glassine, and fumed silica
120 x 600 x 360 in.

documents how dramatically and inventively the artist has transformed his art, and in the process has broken new ground in sculpture.

With the large-scale work that is the focus of the Bellevue Arts Museum exhibition, Grade has introduced a fresh paradigm for art inspired by the earth. His art is not made *from* the land yet resides there for extended periods. It exudes an unmistakable sense of place and circumstance but is not chained to one spot, and instead is adaptable to multiple sitings. Precision crafted, his projects make use of industrial materials and carefully strategized engineering only to be left at the mercy of unpredictable elements that may alter the work in unforeseen ways. The impetus for this art originates as much in literature and the romantic imagination as it does in science and the artist's own confrontations with the hard facts of geology and physics. Grade's sculptural installations have a broad ecological sweep to them and a sense of multiple lives that seems far removed from the excavated, found physicality of works by Smithson and company. As the exhibition's subtitle underscores, Grade creates sculpture *through* landscape; here a poetic, abstract sensibility harnesses the forces of nature to shape surfaces and forms that embody those processes while remaining separate from them. At its core, this is an art that is elemental and itinerant. After this exhibition, too, each work will strike its tent, so to speak, and move on to its next encampment.

Since completing his BFA studies at the Pratt Institute's School of Art and Design in New York, Grade has not been one for limiting his creative life to the studio, hunkering down within its walls to come up with ideas. Typically, rather than continue the academic track by pursuing an MFA, he obtained instead a generous travel grant from Pratt that enabled him to spend an extended period traveling abroad. The destinations he chose to visit are revealing in that they were not those boasting the iconic sites and collections of Western art history. He was seeking new visual experiences, and in countries such as Mexico, Guatemala, Peru, Vietnam, Laos, and India, Grade went off on his own, hiking into remote areas, lured by the unfamiliar and the unexpected, photographing and sketching as he went. He further indulged this impulse with trips to the Middle East, North Africa, and the former Soviet bloc countries of Eastern Europe.

In his continuing determination to get out of the house, Grade has also participated in numerous residencies offered by foundations, such as the Art and Industry Program at the Kohler Arts Center in Wisconsin in 2003, and five residencies since the summer of 2005 from the Pacific Coast to New Hampshire, from the North Rim of the Grand Canyon to the northwest corner of Ireland. Interspersed have been visits to London, Uganda, and weeks at a time in the deserts of Utah, Nevada, and Arizona. Each of these residencies and trips has contributed in one way or another to the conception and/or development of specific works of art.

The diverse geographical, biological, and cultural experiences of his travels in the 1990s collectively provided a wealth of source material that inspired the body of work surveyed in Boise. The sculpture in that exhibition encompassed small-scale pieces presented on pedestals to large, life-size works suspended in space or seemingly sprouting out of the walls and floor. Essentially abstract, they represented biomorphic form in flux, evoking the natural processes of generation or degeneration. Some had anthropomorphic overtones, others an architectonic aspect, with a number insinuating a vague functionality. As composites of plant, animal, and human form, these objects revealed a fascination with the patterns and designs found in nature, and the artist's gift for instilling a sense of awe and mystery. Many of these characteristics have remained crucial elements of Grade's art.

Anecdotes from his numerous travel destinations and foundation residencies tell of events that foreshadowed the sculptural projects currently on view in *Disintegration*. For example, during his travels in several remote, third-world locales Grade left behind sculptures or earthworks made from the indigenous materials at hand as a response to the landscape or a particular aspect of it. Likewise, on Washington State's Olympic Peninsula in 1994 he created the site-specific *Dripper*, which Grade describes as a "perpetual motion piece" propelled by the accumulation of near-constant rainfall there, which sets in motion subsequent sections of the work, lowering and distributing the captured water to the ground.[4] This impulse to make and leave behind works that commemorate the artist's time in a place, that have a private significance rather than a public one, and that interact with and sometimes succumb to the elements—while leaving a subtle imprint too—is one that survives to this day in the new works.

There has long been a narrative element to Grade's art, as each work incorporates some experience in the natural world that triggered it in the first place. However, since 2004 Grade has been especially concerned with carrying a narrative thread through the multiple locations he chooses for his projects. He says his conversations with composers and writers "helped me to think about my sculpture not as static objects with an intended ideal state to preserve, but instead as stories or compositions with an arc, with life . . . "[5]

Unlike the artists of the original earthworks movement, Grade finds his inspiration in communing with nature rather than merely hunting out a site to accommodate or realize an idea. Most often, a place captures his imagination long before he knows what he will do with it, whether this happens while walking on the bogs of Ireland or climbing the glaciers on Mount Rainier. Over the years, Grade has acquired an unusual perspective on landscape, one he is continually refining. As an avid climber and hiker who does not shy from risk-taking, he has spent months exploring the nooks and crannies of harsh terrains, crawling in and out of slender slot canyons and breathtaking glacial crevasses. As a result, Grade has developed a habit of thinking about nature from the inside out, achieving a dual vision that sees not only the surface but what lies beneath it as well (a sixth sense encouraged by his reading of certain poets). As early as his 2000 work *Stem* he was making sculptures that simultaneously presented interior and exterior views of organic subjects. He developed this perspective further in his Boise Art Museum exhibit with his large, horizontal *Caudex* piece (2004). Hanging suspended from the ceiling, it allowed viewers to not only see its strange, mammalian exterior up close but also to experience its interior space, which, with its doubled-over folds and membrane-like construction, felt like peering inside a breathing organism. This idiosyncratic approach to nature became a departure point for several of his large installation works, like the *Seeps of Winter* project at Suyama Space earlier this year, and before that *Cleave*, now reinstalled for this exhibition.

It was during his nomadic period of discovery that Grade also acquired a new appreciation for the relationship of the human body to the earth's surface. He found that exposure to ancient rituals and beliefs involving the body, including burial and entombment practices in places like Peru and Vietnam, awakened in him the deeper implications of the body's intimate relationship with landscape. An esoteric Southeast Asian tribal practice of entombing the deceased in carved-out trunks of old-growth trees for one year, after which the remains are retrieved and the trees allowed to heal, never to be used again,

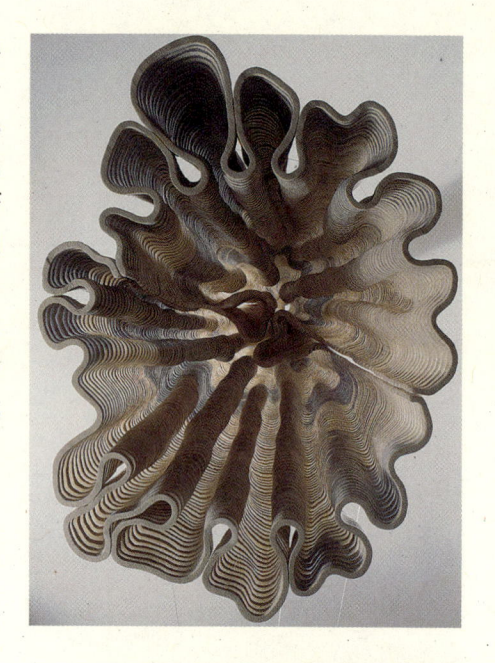

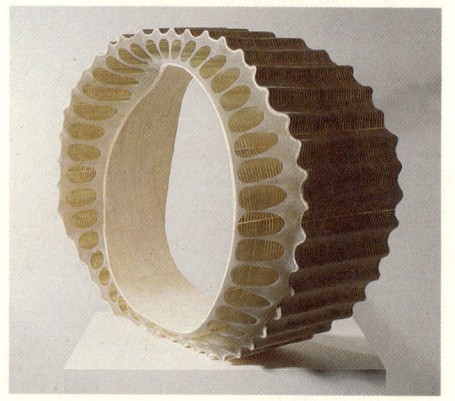

(top)
CAUDEX (HORIZONTAL HALF)
2004
Resin and wood
186 x 24 x 22 in.

(above)
STEM
2000, Wood and resin
30 x 37 x 16 in.

PARED CICATRICE
2003
Cast iron, steel, and acrylic
55 x 36 x 36 in.

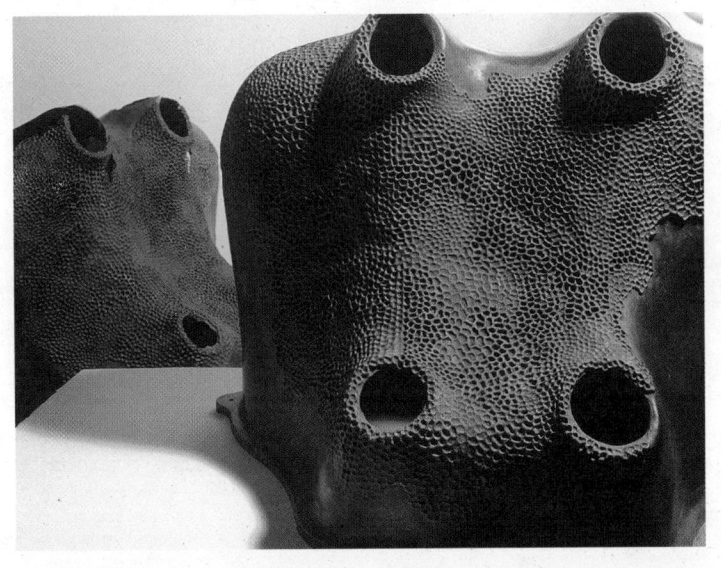

resonated with Grade. The ceremonial restoration of the body to Mother Earth, both symbolically and literally, and the related concept of empty vessels that once held something of value, was the subject of Grade's dark *Pared Cicatrice* sculpture of 2003. Increasingly, and in a variety of ways, a dialogue with the human form became part of the equation he turned to in the formulation of his visual ideas, whether in his earlier anthropomorphic works like *Pared Cicatrice*, or his empathetic communion with Ireland's lost "bog people" in *Seeps of Winter* ("through my fabrics and skins / the seeps of winter / digested me").[6]

The artist's interest in ritual interments tied to landscape is not a morbid one, but it does reflect a neo-romantic sensibility reminiscent of the nineteenth-century German painter Caspar David Friedrich. Friedrich's scenes of snow-covered graveyards and ruined cloisters amid leafless, twisted oaks are well known, but it is in his paintings of dolmens, the pagan graves sealed by megalithic boulders, that we especially find a spirit kindred to Grade's. The moist, misty forest settings of Friedrich's dolmen paintings, *Seeps of Winter*'s tribute to the human compost of the bogs, and the wooded environs of Grade's new work all imply some form of renewal after death. Both artists tap into the basic human yearning that Simon Schama has described as "the craving to find in nature a consolation for our mortality."[7]

The transformation of the human organism into an agent of regeneration is only part of Grade's larger interests, which involve and investigate themes of decay and transition as sculptural processes. Of the new sculpture, *Fold* will be buried to provoke decay through prolonged exposure to desert termites, while both *Collector* and *Host* are premised in part on the notion of contributing to the environment in the course of their decomposition. Clearly, Grade's art represents a reciprocal rather than an impositional approach to landscape.

Cleave, the introductory work in *Disintegration*, deals with transition at a much slower pace. Completed in 2006, this labyrinthine composition is an important piece for Grade, representing his own transition to a new monumentality through an installation that takes to heart the processes that create unique geophysical features. At eleven feet in height and approximately seventeen feet long it allows, and indeed compels the viewer to enter and respond from within, eerily reliving the artist's own confrontation with narrow, water-carved fissures, both glacial and geological. By setting up a dialogue between the body and this composite environment, the artist strove to "humanize" the claustrophobic yet awe-inspiring attributes of these subterranean places. The result is similar to the strong sense of self-awareness one gets when standing within Richard Serra's curved canyons of steel.

With its darkened entrance and curved passageway that denies us a reassuring exit view, *Cleave* reveals itself slowly. Inside, the caked, river-rock-like walls are actually a compos-

CLEAVE (preparatory sketch)
2006
Graphite on paper
13 x 20 in.

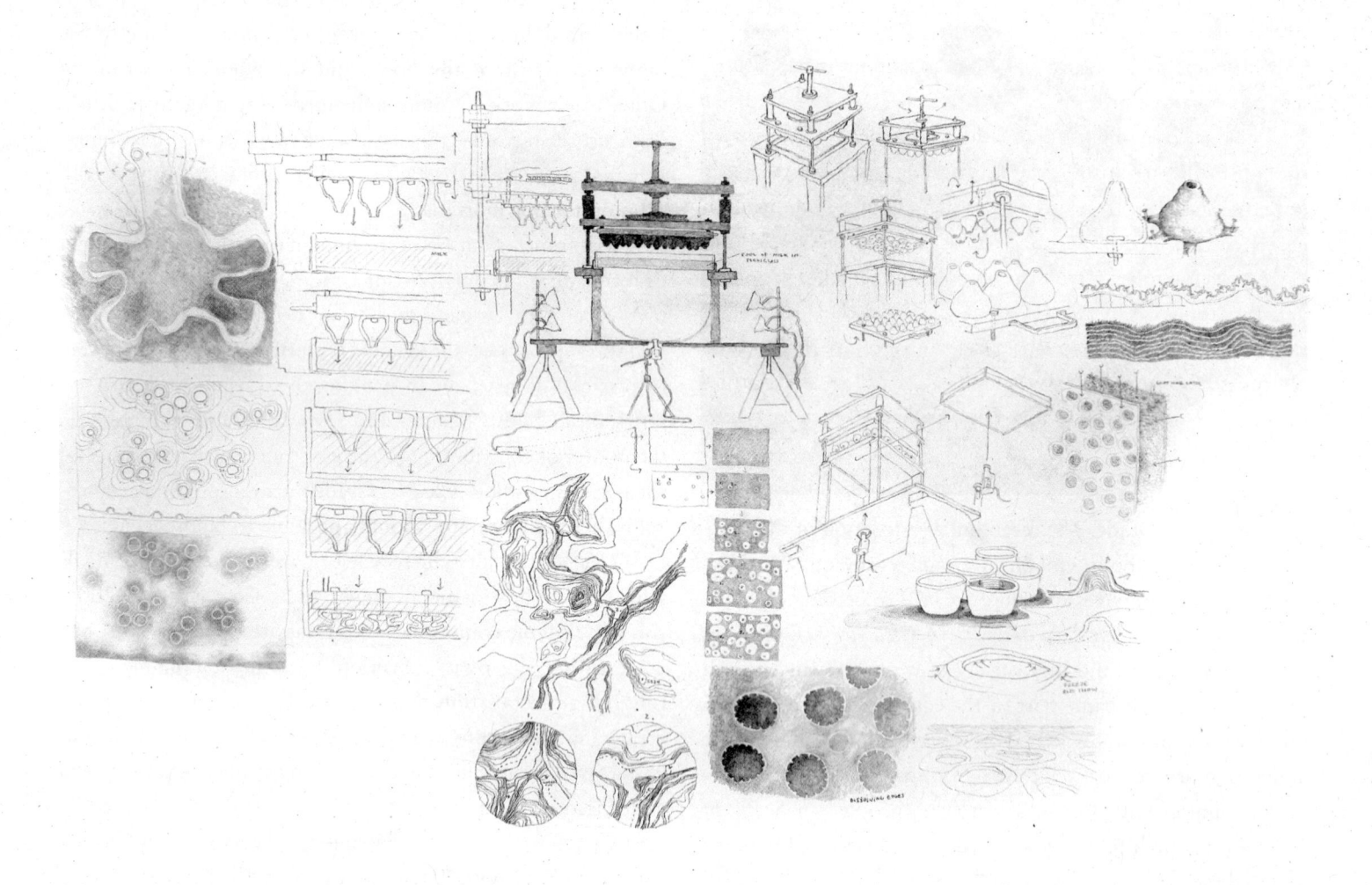

ite of cast resin, clay, and goat fur, methodically subjected to an extended erosive process to evoke a sense of a worn slice of the earth. A staggering amount of material and effort went into accomplishing within a matter of months what would take countless centuries to achieve naturally. Grade coated the translucent cast resin with thousands of pounds of clay mixed with goat hair to create a furlike consistency. After being dried and cured, this surface was subjected to hours of being dowsed with pressurized water, which eroded away much of the clay surface but left the goat hair grafted to the resin, giving the interior the appearance of a long-dry watercourse, and imparting an ancient, airless quality to the interior.

Cleave is actually a multimedia work that brings orchestrated lighting effects and video into the mix as well. Shifting light from above provides the shadow play, while from behind the translucent walls projected video imagery of wet, black clay being immersed in pools of milk creates aureoles of positive and negative space that unevenly illuminate the resin. The work becomes a collage of ice and rock, and intimates a timeless process of change.

Change as a sculptural practice is at the heart of the other four installations in the exhibit. Together, they are a loosely linked series Grade conceived from his readings of mathematician Rene Thom, whose catastrophe theory posits a dichotomy between two types: (1) irreversible, sudden change, or (2) calamity followed by recovery. Grade's idea is that "instead of dividing these types of collapse, I want to overlay them . . . by charting both conditions within the story of one sculptural object."[8] Accomplishing this entails placing each carefully considered and designed work within a pair of successive, often harsh landscape settings, and letting nature take its course. While the two environments he chooses are disparate, they share one or more common elements as well. And sometimes Grade will also assist the process with embedded structural responses to events.

Of the projects in this vein, *Collector* is the first the artist undertook, and, consequently, the one furthest along in its ordeal. Actually, the chronological sequence of this series is very loose, and there can be considerable overlap while he juggles different projects in various stages of development. But Grade's concept of bringing two landscapes to bear on one sculpture first came to fruition here, and, true to form, its story is a complicated one.

To begin with, the title of this work is significant in that collecting mechanisms of all sorts have intrigued Grade since he discovered them in various cultures, such as the pre-Inca funerary towers in Peru. The concept of collecting things—objects, bodies, even sounds and beliefs (both Christian and pagan)—struck a chord in him, and a number of pieces in his 2004 survey embodied this theme. In *Collector*, and in subsequent works, Grade has shifted this interest from a specific cultural context to a hybrid environmental one, allowing this collecting capacity to transform the piece.

Then there is its design. The two halves of *Collector* are long, tapered, horn-shaped structures made of an interlocking latticework of laminated teak wood that fit together to make a six-and-a-half-foot diameter circle. The horn shapes of each half were inspired both by the shape of the longhorns his aunt in Uganda mounted on the front of her truck to ward off bandits (a long story), and by the dimensions of the slot canyon in Utah for which *Collector* was ultimately destined. The latticework enhances the work's sturdiness and collecting abilities in its two intended settings, which, as diverse as they seem, do share one common element: water.

In its first outdoor stage, *Collector* was immersed in the waters of Willapa Bay on the Washington coast beginning in March 2007, where it provided a bed for oysters to collect and grow while also acquiring layers of seaweed, barnacles, and other marine life forms. Lashed with ropes to a metal ring attached to vertical PVC posts in order to secure it during pounding storms (with assistance from the local fishermen, lending a social, community effort element to the project), *Collector* sat semi-submerged for a year until it was retrieved this spring, an occasion celebrated by Grade and his local crew with an on-site oyster harvest and feast.

The transition to the second stage was potentially part of the process too. For the trek down to the southern Utah desert, the horns of *Collector* were secured on the roof of Grade's pickup. On the road, much of the seaweed and oyster remains would supposedly be blown off, presumably to be replaced by splattered bugs. During a brief stopover in Boise, Idaho, the artist and I inspected the piece. After ten hours of

(left) *Burial ground at Saar on Bahrain*

(right) Study for *Fold*

driving, *Collector* was still encrusted with barnacles, bits of oyster and mussel shell, and enough dried-on seaweed to give the work a greenish glow in the right light. Grooves had been worn into the hard teakwood where ropes restrained it during the 100 mph winds of a December storm. It was a sculpture with its own, intact natural history.

In Utah, phase two hit a glitch, bringing the elements of chance and the unexpected into play. The slot canyon for which the work was designed was clogged with debris, dumped there by the same spring flash-floods that were supposed to batter *Collector*. So Grade instead built a framework that would hold the circular piece upright in the hot desert air for the birds and insects to pick at it until it is retrieved for the exhibit.

The second installation, *Host*, can in some respects be considered *Collector*'s sister piece. It, too, is a circular sculpture with tapered ends, has a latticework look to it, and interacts with the local wildlife. *Host*, however, is almost twice the size, but rather than strong and sturdy like *Collector* it is quite fragile, vulnerable even to rain, and thus more transitory in nature.

Approximately eleven feet in diameter, *Host* is made of (digestible) cast cellulose covered with ground seeds, with twenty-four telescoping parts, and was sited at two different locations in the Kaibab National Forest just beyond the Grand Canyon's North Rim. Whereas with *Collector* birds became a fallback agent of change, in *Host* they (specifically the desert wren) play an integral role in the work by picking apart the cellulose while eating the seeds.

Grade first installed the linked-together sections in a burned-out swath left by a recent forest fire. The pristine, white cellulose mesh suspended among the fire-blackened tree trunks made for a striking sculptural image. Unfortunately, the birds were not in sight and insects came to feast instead. A week later, Grade moved *Host* to a stand of flourishing Aspens, but this time rodents crowded out the birds. Only after coating the cellulose with a jalapeño pepper derivative was Grade able to keep the squirrels at bay to the advantage of the wrens. After several weeks, *Host* was taken down, and is presented here, to quote the artist, in a state of "arrested development."

Fold and *Meridian* are two new sculptures, fresh from the studio. The skeletal, cell-like structural design of *Fold* is informed by the artist's interest in cell structure as a formal language, as well as the characteristics of exotic hardwoods, and the indented, rectilinear patterns of ancient grave sites in the North African desert. Exhibited upright as an irregular, undulating, eight-foot-diameter cylinder, *Fold* has a translucent resin interior skin supporting its handmade square compartments, which range in size from an eighth of an inch to three inches square, made of two species of hardwood from Central Africa, limba and imbua. The design and materials offer overlapping variables that will direct the intrusion of termites when the work is buried, edge down, in the Nevada desert for two years.

In *Fold*'s buried position, the wood compartments that break through at ground level will form a crenulated edge, allowing light down into the sculpture through the ever-diminishing openings, encouraging the termites to descend into the wood interior which, for half the piece, comes to a folded lip or cul-de-sac, if you will, at the bottom. Of the two wood types Grade chose, limba is light-colored while imbua has a much darker tone. The dark wood, it turns out, attracts the insects, thereby further directing the course of destruction. If all goes according to plan, one lower side of *Fold* should have a blasted-away, pestilential look when it is finally retrieved.

Meridian is probably Grade's most ambitious installation to date in terms of engineering in advance structural changes that will occur during the course of its life in the landscape, giving it a kinetic aspect. It is Grade's most explicit attempt to recreate an overlay of Rene Thom's two types of catastrophe. Twelve feet in length and sixteen feet in diameter at its largest point, *Meridian* contains eleven circular sections, its cylindrical form made up of approximately 350 small, vertebrae-like segments, each one of them housing a strong filament (the "umbilical cord") that extends beyond the exterior of the work. Cast in a composite of thin, translucent rubber, cellulose, urethane foam, and casein, it also has an internal, riblike structure fashioned from a strong, rigid, but lightweight polyurethane used by the Navy for submarine parts. Each segment has a total weight of less than a pound, making it light enough to stay airborne in strong winds.

At the museum, *Meridian* is displayed in a vertical position, a strange, monolithic structure with filaments radiating in all directions like giant feelers. In a slot canyon in Northern Arizona, it will be anchored by water-weighted aluminum camming devices that will secure it to the canyon rim and keep the filaments taut. When the water evaporates, the filaments will release from the anchors, and the interconnected rings will fold in on each other, causing hundreds of lightweight segments to fall into the canyon, suspended on strands of filament "like collapsing marionettes."[9] Grade chose this specific site for its strong updrafts and the winds that funnel through the fissure; periodically they will turn the segments into airborne kites while also entangling them together like the debris that naturally collects in these canyons. These "kites" are protected for collisions with the rock walls by their bumpy, rubber surface (which may eventually get worn away) and by *Meridian*'s interior strength.

For Part II, the sculpture's dangling, entangled mass will be moved intact to a redwood forest on the California coast where it will be installed in a circle of Sequoias, suspended a hundred feet in the air, just below the canopy. There it will be subjected to almost constant rainfall. The combination of rain, which weakens the binding characteristics of some surface materials while intensifying the bonding of others, and the winds, which will have a contorting effect, should cause the sculpture's mass to gradually widen and transform from a vertical to a stretched horizontal form, in effect creating a new horizon line in the site. Over several months it will also collect organic material, fusing into a rigid net of forest and man-made matter. Recovery retrieved from calamity.

Part of the intellectual beauty of Grade's new installation work, one of its most stimulating characteristics, is its open-endedness. For all the research, planning, and workmanship that goes into these sculptural projects, none of them can be considered complete or at the end of the creative process. *Seeps of Winter*, made from cast paper pulp, glassine, and wood, and disassembled at Suyama Space in April, will be moved to a glacier on Mount Baker, in Washington, where it will be mounted upside-down on stakes, to be covered with snow, and through whose holes icicles may form. After it thaws, it will be taken apart and moved again, a soggy and wrinkled bogland. For *Collector*, after the *Disintegration* exhibit, Grade will attempt to find another slot canyon to accommodate its design so it can yet experience the spring flash floods of the desert. And *Host* will be returned to a new stand of trees so birds can reap the benefits of its return to nature. Who knows how many lives and afterlives are in store for *Fold* and *Meridian*?

While these to-be-continued sculptural narratives give Grade's art an elusive quality, they also reflect the balance he strikes between what he gives and what he takes in this aesthetic interchange with the land. Grade goes to great lengths to insure that an idea inspired by nature *works* in nature, and to adhere to a way of making art that is both meaningful and respectful of the environment. What he takes back is the imprint of earth, ice, water, wind, or wildlife that makes these pieces happen in a manner that resonates on a visceral level and recognizes no time restraints. As a consequence these powerful sculptures have an integrity, and an instinctively composed, dignified demeanor commensurate with a timeless process. John Keats's description of the sea eerily captures this core essence of Grade's art: "It keeps eternal whisperings around..."[10]

NOTES

[1] Seamus Heaney, "Glanmore Sonnets," in *Field Work* (New York: Farrar, Straus, Giroux, 1979), p. 33.

[2] Simon Schama, *Landscape and Memory* (New York: Knopf, 1995), pp. 6–7.

[3] Peter Schjeldahl, "Uncluttered," *New Yorker*, April 28, 2008, p. 82.

[4] Audio recording of John Grade interview with Jen Graves of *The Stranger* (Seattle), January 23, 2008.

[5] Email from the artist, June 6, 2008.

[6] Seamus Heaney, "Bog Queen," in *North* (London: Faber and Faber, 1975), pp. 25–27.

[7] Simon Schama, p. 15.

[8] Interview with the artist, April 2008.

[9] Artist's project proposal statement, 2007.

[10] John Keats, "On the Sea," in *John Keats: The Poems* (New York: Knopf, Everyman's Library Edition, 1999), p. 271.

Christopher Schnoor, an art writer and critic based in Boise, Idaho, has written and lectured on Northwest art for over twenty years. His articles, reviews, and essays have appeared in *Art in America, Sculpture, Artweek,* the *Boise Weekly*, and a number of museum publications.

CHECKLIST OF THE EXHIBITION

MERIDIAN

2008

Rubber, fabric, foam, and monofilament

144 x 192 in. diameter

Courtesy of Davidson Galleries and the artist

HOST

2007–2008

Cellulose

12 x 144 in. diameter

Courtesy of Davidson Galleries and the artist

FOLD

2008

Wood and resin

36 x 90 in. diameter

Courtesy of Davidson Galleries and the artist

COLLECTOR

2007

Wood

8 x 72 x 78 in.

Courtesy of Davidson Galleries and the artist

CLEAVE

2006

Clay, goat fur, resin, and video projection

156 x 45 x 288 in.; interior passage approximately

123 x 26 x 184 in.

Courtesy of Davidson Galleries and the artist

DRAWINGS

O

2006

Graphite on paper

4 x 7 in.

Driek and Michael Zirinsky Collection

BETWEEN TURF FACE AND DEMESNE WALL

2005

Charcoal on paper

46 x 104 in.

Tacoma Art Museum; Gift of the Artist

CLEAVE (preparatory sketch)

2006

Graphite on paper

13 x 20 in.

Private collection

JOHN GRADE

Born: Minneapolis, 1970; lives and works in Seattle, Washington

Education: Pratt Institute, Brooklyn, NY (BFA, 1992)

SELECTED SOLO EXHIBITIONS

2008   Davidson Galleries, Seattle, WA

Bellevue Arts Museum, Bellevue, WA. Catalogue.

Suyama Space, Seattle, WA. Catalogue.

2007   Seattle Art Museum Gallery, Seattle, WA

2006   Davidson Contemporary, Seattle, WA

2005   Davidson Galleries, Seattle

King County Performance Network, King County, WA

2004   Davidson Galleries, Seattle

John Grade: Sculpture and Drawings. Boise Art Museum, Boise, ID. Catalogue.

2003   Davidson Galleries, Seattle

2002   Davidson Galleries, Seattle

2000   Laura Russo Gallery, Portland, OR
Davidson Galleries, Seattle
King County Art Gallery, Seattle

SELECTED GROUP EXHIBITIONS

2007   *Northwest Biennial*, Tacoma Art Museum, Tacoma, WA. Catalogue.

Davidson Contemporary, Seattle

2006   SPUR Projects, Portola Valley, CA

Concord Art Association, Concord, MA. Catalogue.

John Michael Kohler Arts Center, Sheboygan, WI

Aqua Art, Miami, FL

2005   Bumbershoot Visual Arts Exhibition, Seattle. Catalogue.

San Francisco International Art Exhibition, Fort Mason, San Francisco, CA

Aqua Art, Miami

2004   John Michael Kohler Arts Center, Sheboygan. Catalogue.

San Francisco International Art Exhibition, Fort Mason, San Francisco

John Michael Kohler Arts Center, Sheboygan

2002   Davidson Galleries, Seattle

Pratt Manhattan Gallery, New York City. Catalogue.

San Francisco International Art Exhibition, Fort Mason, San Francisco

Bumbershoot Visual Arts Exhibition, Seattle

2001   Davidson Galleries, Seattle

2000   Bellevue Art Museum, Bellevue, WA. Catalogue.

Laura Russo Gallery, Portland, OR

Boise Art Museum, Boise, ID

Bellevue Sculpture Exhibition, Meydenbauer Center, Bellevue, WA

1999   Davidson Galleries, Seattle

Bumbershoot Visual Arts Exhibition, Seattle. Best of Show Award.

Bellevue Art Museum, Bellevue

AWARDS

2008 Grant, 4Culture, King County Project Grant, Seattle

Grant, City of Seattle, Mayor's Office of Arts and Cultural Affairs, City Artists Program, Seattle

2007 Grant, Artist Trust Foundation, GAP program, Seattle

Grant, 4Culture, King County Project Grant, Seattle

2005 Grant, Pollock-Krasner Foundation, New York City

Fellowship, Louis Comfort Tiffany Foundation, New York City

Grant, 4 Culture, King County Performance Network, Seattle

2004 Grant, Andy Warhol Foundation for the Visual Arts, New York City

Grant, 4Culture, King County Project Grant, Seattle

Grant, City of Seattle: Mayor's Office of Arts and Cultural Affairs, City Artists Program, Seattle

Grant, Artist Trust Foundation, GAP program, Seattle

2003 Fellowship, Washington State Arts Commission and Artist Trust Foundation, WA

1999 Grant, Artist Trust Foundation, GAP program, Seattle

1994 Grant, Middleditch Graduation Travel Award, Pratt Institute, Brooklyn, NY

1992 Departmental Distinction for Achievement in Drawing, Pratt Institute, Brooklyn, NY

1988 National Talent Search Foundation Full-Tuition Scholarship, Pratt Institute, Brooklyn

RESIDENCIES

2007 MacDowell Colony, Peterborough, NH. (Gottlieb Foundation Endowed Fellowship)

National Park Service, Grand Canyon, North Rim, AZ

2006 Espy Foundation, Oysterville, WA

2005 Ballenglen Arts Foundation, Ballycastle, County Mayo, Ireland

Djerassi Foundation, Woodside, CA. (Pritzker Foundation Endowed Fellowship)

2003 John Michael Kohler Arts Center and Foundry, Arts/Industry Program, Sheboygan

SELECTED REVIEWS, INTERVIEWS, AND PUBLICATIONS

2008 Farr, Sheila. "Hot Ticket: John Grade at Suyama Space." *Seattle Times*, March 21.

Grant, Adriana. "Seeps of Winter Could Make You Sick." *Seattle Weekly*, February 13.

Graves, Jen. "The Roaming Sculptures of John Grade." *The Stranger*, January 23.

Hackett, Regina. "Best Bet: John Grade." *Seattle Post-Intelligencer*, March 21.

Moyer, Twylene. "Itinerary: John Grade, Suyama Space." *Sculpture*, March.

Simonini, Ross. " 'Seeps' Is on a Fascinating Path to Destruction." *Seattle Post-Intelligencer*, March 5.

2007 Gardener, Jan. "One Hundred Years and Change." *Boston Globe*, February 10.

Silverman, Art. "Artists Retreat into Solitude." *All Things Considered*, National Public Radio, March 5.

2006 Curtis, Molly Norris. "Make the Grade." *Art Access*, June.

Hackett, Regina. "Best Bet." *Seattle Post-Intelligencer*, May 19.

Louis Comfort Tiffany Awards 2005 catalogue, Tiffany Foundation, New York City.

Pence, Elizabeth, "John Grade." *ArtUS*, October.

Schnoor, Christopher. "Cleavage." *Boise Weekly*, July 5.

Stracener, Brad. "Artist Finds Inspiration Inside Crevasse." *Mountaineer*, April.

2005 Farr, Sheila. "A Unified Group of Exhibitions." *Seattle Times*, September 2.

Koplos, Janet. "Report from Seattle: Plugged in and Caffeinated." *Art in America*, September.

Schnoor, Christopher. "Review: John Grade at Boise Art Museum." *Art in America*, September.

Sexton, Brenda. "Art on Display." *Enumclaw Courier-Herald*, front page, September 28.

Van Nostrand, Jess. *Raw and Refined*. Bumbershoot Visual Arts exhibition catalogue, Seattle

2004 Kangas, Matthew. "Review: John Grade at Davidson Galleries." *Sculpture*, September.

———. "Excursions and Interventions," in *John Grade: Sculpture and Drawings*, Boise, ID: Boise Art Museum.

Oland, Dana. "Art Lesson." *Idaho Statesman (Boise)*, August 19.

———. "John Grade: An Artist on the Verge." *Idaho Statesman*, August 19.

Schnoor, Christopher. "Art in Flux: John Grade's World at Boise Art Museum." *Boise Weekly*, November 10.

2003 Bullis, Douglas, ed. *100 Artists of the West Coast*. Atglen, PA: Schiffer Books.

Frank, Hillary. "John Grade Interview: Artists Working in Industry." *Studio 360* program, National Public Radio, broadcast June 14.

2002 Daftari, Fereshteh. *Pratt Alumni*. Exhibition catalogue. Brooklyn, NY: Pratt Institute.

2000 Boas, Pat. "John Grade at Laura Russo Gallery." *Artweek*, July.

Byrne, Mary. *Bellevue Sculpture*. Exhibition catalogue. Bellevue, WA: Bellevue Arts Commission.

Ellison, Victoria. "Up-and-Coming Sculptor." *Seattle Weekly*, April 20.

Fahey, Anne. "Show and Tell." *Seattle Weekly*, August 17.

Hackett, Regina. "Art in Progress." *Seattle Post-Intelligencer*, July 11.

Hall, Emily. "Bio: Art: John Grade." *The Stranger*, November 23.

———. "The Better Annual." *The Stranger*, July 20.

Josslin, Victoria. "Loss, Disintegration and Nostalgia at the Davidson Galleries." *Seattle Post-Intelligencer*, November 11.

BELLEVUE ARTS MUSEUM

BOARD OF TRUSTEES 2008

President: Susan Edelheit

Carol Auerbach
Keith Gormley Baldwin
Ron Bayley
Sherry Benaroya
Al Berger
Richard Collette
Manya Drobnack
Alexandra Muse Ehrlich
John Frank
Lawrence Hebner
John Hepler
Anne Kilcup
Norma Klorfine
Larry Metcalf
Valerie Piha
Kevin Schemm
Pat Smith
Angela Sutter
Cappy Thompson
Susan Thurston

Docent President: Marsha Freeny
Docent Representative: Miriam Charney
Guild Representative: Yvonne Miller

STAFF

Michael Monroe *Executive Director and Chief Curator*

Tanja Baumann *Director of Marketing and Public Relations*

Stefano Catalani *Curator*

Renate Raymond *Deputy Director*

Marguerite Stanley *Chief Financial Officer and Director of Human Resources*

Lawrence Asmann *Facility Manager*
Nora Atkinson *Exhibitions Curator*
Madison Brewton *Guest Services*
Chanta Chhay *Membership Manager*
Amanda Chilsholm *Guest Services*
Barbara DiFerrante *Retail Buyer*
Ester Fajzi *Registrar*
Jessica Glover *Retail Store Manager*
Sayaka Ito *Marketing Coordinator and Webmaster*
Ken Kelly *Facilities Assistant*
Meredith Langridge *Assistant Fair Manager and Education Coordinator*
Donna Lundquist *Graphic Designer*
Jolie Maki *Retail Sales Associate*
Patrick McMahon *Education Curator*
Kathleen Pendleton *Special Events and Volunteer Coordinator*
Marta Sivertsen *Assistant Preparator*
John Thomas *Retail Sales Associate*
Elisabeth Wahlers *Arts Fair and Patron Party Manager*
Vincent Warner *Head Preparator*
Lyn Ziskind *Retail Sales Associate*

Published in conjunction with the exhibition
John Grade: Disintegration, Sculpure through Landscape
organized by Bellevue Arts Museum, August 26 – November 30, 2008.

All dimensions are given in inches, height precedes width precedes depth.

Copyright © 2008 by Bellevue Arts Museum.

ISBN: 978-0-942342-17-8

All rights reserved. No part of this book may be reproduced or transmitted in any form or by any means, electronic or mechanical, including photocopy, recording, or any other information storage and retrieval system without permission in writing from Bellevue Arts Museum.

Director Michael W. Monroe
Curator Stefano Catalani
Editing by Sigrid Asmus
Design by Phil Kovacevich

All photos by John Grade except as noted.
Nora Atkinson, p. 58; Mark Bauschke, p. 34 (left);
Maria Grade: cover, pp. 2, 26 (right), 46; Robert Harding World Imagery, p. 72 (left); Richard Nicol: back cover, pp. 14, 15, 16, 19, 20, 21, 38, 41, 42, 43, 44, 45, 47, 48, 50, 52.

Published by Bellevue Arts Museum, Bellevue, Washington.
Printed and bound in Canada by Friesens Book Division.

Bellevue Arts Museum illuminates and enriches the human spirit through art, craft and design.

BELLEVUE ARTS MUSEUM
510 Bellevue Way
Bellevue WA 98004
Phone (425) 519-0770
Fax (425) 637-1799
E-mail info@bellevuearts.org
www.bellevuearts.org

This exhibition and accompanying publication is made possible with generous support from:

Additional support for the realization of the sculptures featured in the exhibition has been provided by:

Louis Comfort Tiffany Foundation, Pollock-Krasner Foundation, U.S. National Park Service, MacDowell Colony, Espy Foundation